Under The Edge
The Architecture of
Peter Stutchbury

Edited by Ewan McEoin
Photography by Michael Nicholson
First published by the Architecture Foundation Australia

Thames & Hudson

First published in Australia in 2011 by
the Architecture Foundation Australia.
Second edition published in 2015.
Architecture Foundation Australia
PO Box 90
Brooklyn NSW 2083
info@ozetecture.org
www.ozetecture.org

This edition first published by Thames &
Hudson Australia Pty Ltd in 2016.
11 Central Boulevard Portside Business Park
Port Melbourne VIC 3207
ABN: 72 004 751 964

www.thameshudson.com.au

ISBN: 9780500500699

Cataloguing-in-Publication entry is available
from the National Library of Australia:
http://catalogue.nla.gov.au/

Editor: Ewan McEoin
Photography: Michael Nicholson
Art direction and design: Studio Round
Editorial co-ordinator: Lindsay Johnston
Printing: Everbest Printing Co Ltd

Cover image: Contour House, Berry
Mountain, NSW, 2011 / Cover illustration:
Sketch by Peter Stutchbury
Previous page: Aboriginal Elder Uncle
Max Dulumunmun Harrison welcomes
Peter Stutchbury to the land of his
people in a traditional smoke ceremony.
Photo: Jure Zavrtanik

Contents

Lindsay Johnston
33°39'03"S 151°18'40"E

Lindsay Johnston is Convenor of the Architecture Foundation Australia and former Head of School and Dean of the Faculty of Architecture, Building and Design, at the University of Newcastle, Australia.

The architecture of the Edge, architecture of the Asia Pacific Antipodes, may be a counter-proposition to the mainstream architecture of the developed world.

In order to understand one's self, it is illuminating to attempt to understand the opposite, and it is for this reason that the architecture, particularly of Australia, the biggest land-mass in the Antipodes, now attracts such international interest.

There is an historical interface here between the hegemony of western culture and the many and exotic cultures of the east, of the Pacific Islands and the, perhaps misnamed, 'primitive' indigenous cultures, that exposes a deep understanding of building in harmony with place, climate and nature. The leading Australian environmentalist Bill Mollison, in his books on 'Permaculture', postulates "The seemingly-wild and naturally-functioning garden of a New Guinea villager is beautifully ordered and in harmony, while the clipped lawns and pruned roses of the pseudo-aristocrat are nature in wild disarray."

Australian architecture has grown from frugality, from scarce resources – either as indigenous building or the building of the early European settlers – thus giving it an integrity without flourish, that is technically considered. Unlike so much European architecture, it is not based on mass for substance and stability, but on a fragile framed typology in timber and, later, steel that defines much of the architecture of today. Technology that is efficient, often informed by nautical skills, derived from immediate and transportable materials and, interestingly, capable of disassembly and reuse – a contemporary imperative.

A benign climate in many parts of Australia facilitates dissolution of the boundary between inside and out, manifest architecturally in walls that slide completely away, corners that fold out and, even, roofs that open to the sky - buildings that can be 'sailed like a yacht'. Thus setting up an immediacy between architecture and place, users and climate, that is 'news' to many from other parts of the globe and is timely, now, in the contemporary global challenge to reduce resource consumption by the human species on planet Earth.

Brit Andresen

Foreword

Peter Stutchbury's award winning architecture continues to stimulate a new and increasing awareness of the potential for designing with the Australian landscape and its environment. His built works of architecture are expertly and inventively responsive to the environmental context in both form and technology. Many works have that added quality of being composed with a 'knowing anticipation' of movement through spaces that offers memorable experiences of the landscape. Carefully constructed openings are located to expand compressed space but also to offer an experience of the natural world both through near views of great rocks close by and distant views up to animated treetops and shifting sky.

His exemplary architecture also exhibits the way technology may be adopted and elegantly transformed to meet the more complex performance tasks of shelter and context. It demonstrates great clarity of thinking in adapting a range of passive cooling methods to moderate the impact of a challenging climate for owners and occupants. This suite of measures, together with creative use of materials and construction simplicity, informs the elegant re-interpretation of iconic Australian building typologies. Whilst Peter Stutchbury's knowledge and respect for traditional building methods contribute to his analytical thinking, it is his formal and technical synthesis in designing which has reinvigorated and transformed the traditional to produce both exceptional contemporary buildings and new models for living and working.

With his open-minded and experimental approach to architecture, Peter Stutchbury has engaged with and completed many inter-cultural commissions of high merit including projects in Australia, Russia and Japan. His ongoing interest in inter-cultural and international exchanges finds expression not only in his practice work, the make-up of his studio team and professional presentations but also in his involvement with architectural education and general architectural culture-building. Through his lecturing and teaching both in Australia and abroad, Peter Stutchbury has been a central figure in introducing international students of architecture to issues inherent in designing with the Australian landscape and in promoting the highest standards of architecture.

Brit Andresen is a distinguished academic and Emeritus Professor at the University of Queensland. As a practitioner, with her partner Peter O'Gorman, their works have been published internationally. She was the first female recipient of the Gold Medal of the Australian Institute of Architects in 2002.

Viewing aperature overlooking the surf break at Theatre House, Central Coast, NSW.

Detail of roof vents at Reef House, Vanuatu, tuned to capture prevailing sea breezes and cross-ventilate the house.

Richard Leplastrier
The Land in Mind

Home: no roads here – only boats – this waterbourne community. About 1974. Sitting alone quietly on this dilapidated deck. Looking out over the estuary, fine ruffles of wind on water, skeined fingers of reflection. The sand spit – this time tide clock a perfect taper of forces. Mind wandering.

Peace broken by sudden arrival of a ginger border collie, tongue hanging out. It's summer. Followed by this young bloke, also unannounced, leaning forward slightly, medium height, lightly but strongly built, fair hair in ponytail, bare foot, blue stubbies and Jacky Howe singlet. Maybe Scandinavian. 'Sorry to interrupt.' Who is this young fella - didn't I see him recently – ah yes, that wedding up in Newcastle, me soaking wet after motorcycle ride through severe storm. Came straight up to me, he did – no intro – 'hey, I've seen that house in the walled palm garden that you're doing and how're you going to sort out that giant dish gutter over the gallery why don't you do this....' All in one sentence, no stopping for my answer. As I remember his idea wasn't so hot but here he was again - no lack of confidence, straight up front.

This series of mental notes when I first met Stutch, nearly forty years ago. The beginning of a long and sustaining friendship – working, teaching and raising families together. Peter Stutchbury is a northern beaches boy – East Coast Australia. Meaning, surf culture, living outdoors on the ocean margins, a rugged terrain meeting the Tasman Sea in a necklace of beaches between headlands stretching from Manly in the south to the hammer head of Barrenjoey to the north. A climate tempered by the south flowing warm East Coast current. This gives Sydney its subtropical nature. Ideal for stripped back living. The life of these surfers, wandering up and down the coast in an old station wagon or ute, boards on the top or in the back – camping wherever. No, not wherever – but carefully selecting a place for base camp and of course as an architect this is where it all begins. The minimal lifestyle in the best place that nature offers. And you must be discerning and selective.

Concurrent with this was his time spent (and still spent) 450 miles inland across the Great Divide and in the red earth desert fringe country - Cobar. This sheep farming family is on his gentle mother's side. They have great knowledge of the land, its sparse resources and its fierce dynamics. Here he discovered remnants of Aboriginal inhabitation thousands of years old in the rock overhangs of the 'drawers' which emerge from the expansive plain like the arching backbones of giant animals. These caves admit welcome winter sun and have prospect over the open ground for game. The indigenous idea of 'house' extends over an entire landscape, simply moving about from best place to best place as things change through the season. I've seen Stutch's beautiful drawings of this terrain. They are studies which breed an understanding of site, its force of circumstance, circum-stance: that which stands around a place.

The first step in architecture springs from the land, as do the origins of most of our cities. Copenhagen 'trading harbour' – the old beach, protected, where they pulled their boats up to exchange goods. Paris from the defendable 'Îsle de la Cité' in the Seine. Sydney from its secure harbour with its productive margins and midden platforms, and so on. The force of the land is always underlying. We can see this in the pages that follow.

— — Richard Leplastrier is a seminal figure in Australian architecture. He received national recognition in 1999 through the award of the Gold Medal of the Australian Institute of Architects. Richard has received international recognition through receipt of the 2004 'Spirit of Nature Wood Architecture Award' in Finland. He has been awarded the Dreyer Foundation Prize of Honour 2009 in Denmark, the first time an architect from outside Denmark has received this prize.

Many works, each in the same way singular and beautiful and testing the edges. They all have the land in mind.

His studio is a young creative team who are thrown in at the deep end. They are given responsibility from the outset and in the background two brilliant, resourceful, experienced men. Nielsen Warren, a sharp, ethical intelligence with decades of practice behind him. He manages to keep the ship on course. And Professor Max Irvine, structural engineer par excellence and father confessor to many of us. He manages to keep the rig aloft. They give the younger ones confidence and give Peter the room to move to move the room. Now in his fifth decade he's been through over thirty years of practice, the joys and the fires of family (which slaps Purscwarden's poultice on the ego) and he's coming into his most creative years. We all look forward to that.

—

Richard Leplastrier

Ingerid Helsing Almaas

Available Realities

A few comments on the architecture of Peter Stutchbury, offered from Oslo, Norway on 59°56'58"N 10°45'23"E. It is the month of February, 2011, and the temperature is -14°C.

For every thing, statement, occurrence or phenomenon that seems at first glance totally beyond comprehension, there is a reality in which it makes sense. As we walk through life, we pass in and out of a stream of different and wildly incompatible situations, and the only connection between them is the tenuous thread spun by our perception as we go: our ability to make our lives into a believable story. This can be hard work. And when we leave this earth, our story is extinguished; everything we have seen and understood lingers for a moment only, like smoke on the air breathed by the people who were closest to us – and then it is gone.

Unless, of course, we have been sharing our stories with others.

In that case, we might find them settling in the growing sediments of shared culture; our insights, passed on to others or fixed in work we have left behind, slowly ossifying into common patterns of understanding or, perhaps, even hardened into the folded fossils of truth. In our meetings with all these different realities, so many things are available to us. The world offers it all, and our body receives it: the wind, the sun, heat and cold, the ground under our feet, the sound of trickling water or the hum of wheels, the shouts and laughter of people. The continuities of untouched landscapes and the mirror fragments of a city – we move through it all, and everything we meet is open, ours for the taking. Our choice is what we take. What we choose to see, and what, if anything, we choose to do about it. For an architect, this choice is of acute importance, for they will be fixed for many years to come and will present the world to other people in a certain way. Architecture channels our experience; it stands in the way and directs our bodies, opens and closes the world to us in the particular place where a building is built.

But in Australia, things are often not what they appear to be.

Peter Stutchbury's buildings are in many ways deceptive. Seen from Europe, they appear in our magazines and on our web pages, and they look very much at home amongst the modern villas of California or the Mediterranean. We have seen it already – decks and terraces with large areas of glass opening onto lovely vistas of treetops and far hills, a glint of the sea in the distance; gleaming hardwood structures, polished concrete, bespoke steelwork and minimal detailing. A swimming pool. A piece of art or two hinting at a cultured clientele. Ah, we say, look; they do it in Australia too. Nice. The houses – for so far his work comprises mostly houses – sit there in their pictures, aesthetic objects framed and packaged ready for international consumption. They look at home in that international setting, at ease with the red carpets and flashing cameras, the fast and gluttonous appetites of the architectural media.

"My formative years were spent on a 100 000 acre sheep farming property and as a surfer, chasing the best ocean wave around Australia", says Stutchbury, reinforcing the popular image of a white Caucasian male, recently arrived and skimming the swell of history along the edges of an ancient continent, windswept and smiling. We picture the rising dust as his huge flocks of sheep move across the outback, their hard little hooves pounding the ground. Australia – a country of rugged types, wrenching living and leisure from an unwilling and untameable land.

Ingerid Helsing Almaas is an architect and a writer. She lives in Oslo, Norway and is the Editor of *Arkitektur N*, the Norwegian Review of Architecture.

Wall House, Shizuoka, Japan

Early surfing and camping trips, chasing waves around Australia.

Farm education.

Introduced from Europe, sheep are poorly adapted to the fragile Australian landscape.

Beyond the photogenic elegance, these buildings offer connections to place, retreat, coolness and volumes for living.

A photograph cannot fully convey the sound of wind through eucalypts or the shifting smells as the sun and shadow move through the day.

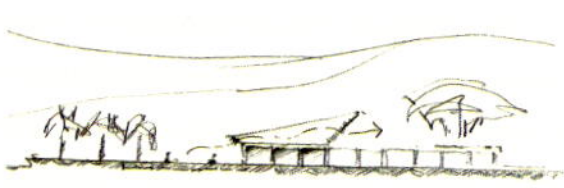

A sustainable house uses naturally occurring processes to maximise the comfort levels of the internal environment for its human inhabitants.

A building site is a combination of elements – sun, wind, water, air, rock, soil, vegetation, animal life.

In fact, the extremities of climate and geography make the Australian ecologies very fragile. All indigenous animals in Australia have soft feet. The soil that is compacted by the hoofed animals that the Europeans brought no longer absorbs the seasonal rain but sheds it, causing flooding and topsoil erosion. The consequences of even small changes to the on-going ecological processes can be as disastrous in the long term as they are hard to spot at first. So, Stutchbury's buildings may look like objects; but in fact they are not. Or, rather, they are much more. The soft-footed structures that his practice has produced are not simply another round of lovely villas – behind their familiar and enticing simplicity, there is something else, something altogether different going on.

The photographs in this book are like a series of mug shots of singers, or craftsmen, or athletes – their faces don't show you what they do. The photograph is incapable of communicating what this entity, this building, is really about. You cannot photograph moving air. You cannot photograph the effect a 20 degree drop in temperature in the scorching heat of the outback; the image will not show the relief of shade on an Australian mid-summer day, the coolness of concrete or the hot breath lifting the air beneath a sheet of corrugated steel. The photograph does not have the patience to wait through the day to feel the difference as windows and panels are opened and closed around the house, letting breezes in or shutting the sun out; or wait for the low mid-winter sun to reach the far wall of a room, gently heating the floor underfoot. It will not convey to the readers of this book the sound of a southerly wind through the eucalypts or the shifting smells as the sun and shadow move across water or grass outside a glass panel slid wide open. Because this is not an architecture of images; each of these houses engage with the site they are in, in ways that cannot be conveyed by photography. Though they may look good in a magazine, that is not where their stories run; that is not the reality in which they make sense.

A sustainable house is a house that does not waste energy in shutting natural processes out and maintaining stable interior environments by artificial means. A sustainable house uses up a minimum of resources in its construction, it causes a minimum of interruptions to, or preferably improves, the natural processes of its site and can be demolished and removed with a minimum of effort, leaving few traces. A sustainable house uses naturally occurring processes to maximise the comfort levels of the internal environment for its human inhabitants. None of these things can be accurately documented in photographs. A photograph can show a deep roof overhang or a discreetly placed solar convector system, but it will not tell you how well these devices work. As a consequence, many people will never know or understand what sustainability in architecture can be, and that it is not primarily visual, that it has only very little to do with anything about architecture that you can see.

In terms of sustainability, it is in fact more accurate to talk about a house sitting in its site than on it. A building site is not just a piece of ground. It consists of a number of different processes that come together in a specific place – sun, wind, water in the air and in the soil, vegetation, animal life. And a building site exists not only in space but also in time: It comprises the changes of day and night, the shifts in weather and the different seasons; in fact, Aboriginal Australians divide the year into nine seasons rather than the four that Europeans are familiar with, and then there are the cycles that are longer than a year, stretching over three years, or five, or sixty... Again, Australia challenges engrained

European perceptions. Nature, here, is not a place: Nature is something that happens.

To make an architecture that engages with and makes good use of all that a site offers, requires knowledge. The white male, living off his acres of sheep and spending his time surfing, could so easily divorce himself from both soil and season. And many European Australians since first encountering the inhospitable effects of the main seasons of the continent – the searing heat of the Dry and the drenching, flooded Wet – have retreated from the land and the incomprehensible climate into sealed, air-conditioned and heated homes, maintaining at a ridiculous environmental expense the illusions of the temperate European climate from whence they and their culture came. But then, there is always someone who opens the door and goes out. And there, of course, are the realities of Australia.

The experience of the land, and ways of dealing with it and adapting to it, is at the heart of Peter Stutchbury's architecture, and the knowledge these buildings display of how to bring together natural processes and human needs is based not only on personal, physical experience, but also on Peter's intimate engagement with Aboriginal culture. The Aboriginal Australians, of course, have used and shaped the landscapes of their continent for thousands of years before the Europeans arrived. And just as many European Australians have separated themselves from the Aboriginals by a number of tactics, from a kind of disinterested cultural air-conditioning to outright and violent racism, so here, too, there will always be someone, somewhere, who opens a door.

Western Europeans tend to emphasise the separation that seems to exist between themselves and the so-called indigenous cultures, the people who have always been there. The gap of technology and of economy seems unbridgeable, widened by language and by mutually incomprehensible habits. And yet, we inhabit the same time. We live together, and we can very easily make our knowledge and experience and explanations of thc world availablc to onc another. "We became friends", says Peter Stutchbury, as he explains how he first met "Uncle" Max Dulumunmun Harrison, an Aboriginal Elder of the Yuin people of New South Wales. It's as simple as that. "Uncle Max has continued to guide me in the Aboriginal ways of respect." Of course. That's what a friend would do. "These ways are not foreign to us as Caucasians, but they have been buried under other, more selfish values."

In his lectures, Peter Stutchbury opens with an explanation – no, a story – of the Aboriginal understanding of the landscape of Australia. He shows a sketch of an Aboriginal house. This house is not a built structure, but a number of places in the small and specific landscape of a little hill. You might walk right through it and not even see it, unless you knew what to look for. The functions of everyday life are laid out in a number of carefully selected spots along and between two rock escarpments. Here, higher up under an overhang retaining the heat of the sun, sleeping. Here, lower down in the shade, cooking and eating. Here, away from animals and insects, storage. Down here the stream for water, over there the trees for midday shade. Beyond, this season's hunting grounds, and soon the fruits of new growth in the woodland cleared by carefully managed bushfires. The distribution of functions move along the rocks, from cave to cave with the light and heat of the day, from shade to shade as the sun moves, and the natural formations and vegetation give shelter and separation as it suits the different activities, ranging from the purely practical to the mysteries of Aboriginal religion.

– – 'Uncle' Max Dulumunmun Harrison

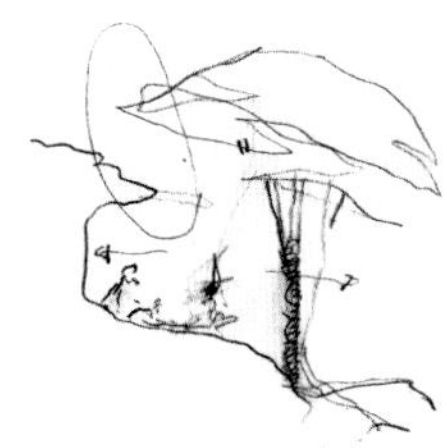

– – In an Aboriginal 'house' the distribution of functions can move along rocks, from cave to cave with the light and heat of the day, from shade to shade as the sun moves, and the natural formations and vegetation give shelter and separation.

Bangalay, Kangaroo Valley, NSW.

Contour House, Bery Mountain, NSW.

Although a building envelope provides structure and enclosure, it can remain open with disintegrating boundaries and multiple functions.

This image of the placement of the activities of daily life according to the natural amenities offered by a given site is a clue to the understanding of Peter's own houses. So to understand them, you need to at least know something about who they are for, about the clients and their preferences, and you need to know something about the local climate – sun angles, orientation, the directions and habits of wind, rain and bushfires, the constitution of the soil and the trees that grow on it. Only then can you understand the shape of the Bangalay House, the main roof raised to catch cooling breezes coming up the valley and the deep lower eaves that shade the glazed elevation; the distribution of light and dense materials in the slab, the massive core and the recycled timber superstructure, placed not just to frame space but to absorb and distribute heat, to even out the fluctuations, warming the winter nights and cooling the summer days. And the long line of the entrance wall of the Berry Mountain 'Contour House', closed to the winds, the sun and the threat of wildfire coming over the crest of the hill to the west, open to the shade of the eastern view through the treetops.

The placement of the functions within these dynamic microclimates depends on the preferences of the client – how much space they need and for what, and where and when they prefer to work, rest, eat or sleep. And although the shape of the house seems closed, resembling the finite envelope of European houses, the structures can always open, functions and activities moving in and out through walls and boundaries as freely as the air and the light. Like the Aboriginal house, life here moves around a number of different places, inside and out, the rooms and terraces opening and closing, shifting their orientation according to the time of day and year. These houses are best described with verbs, not with adjectives. The resulting structures look elegant, of course, and Stutchbury and his team do a flawless job in the detailing and finishing of bolted joints, slender steel mullions and sliding doors. But the real elegance is not something seen: the real elegance of these buildings occurs, as you sit at the table on a sheltered terrace, the Australian midwinter chill softened by the sun captured in the concrete slab underfoot, or the midsummer heat relieved by the same concrete, now cool from the night. This is not the elegance of Caucasian or European culture, formalised and ritualised; Australian elegance is dynamic, it is found in the precise responses borne by the experience and sensitivity of the Aboriginals to their land, translated into the forms and actions of western architectural construction. Nature, here, is something that happens, and so buildings, too, are occurrences rather than objects, and as they shift, turn and open as nature and human life move though them, architecture itself becomes a verb.

In the rationalised responses and precise choices traced in the right angles of thin steel or timber, Peter Stutchbury's structures draw on a detailed understanding of landscape and climate that was not imported from England, nor did it spring from the technological developments of how Western culture in general has dealt with the Australian climate over the past couple of centuries. This understanding is home grown, and it is the result of a number of different and disparate influences, ancient and modern. "Unlike so much European architecture, Australian architecture is not based on mass for substance and stability, but on a fragile framed typology in timber and, later, steel that defines much of the architecture of today," says architect and critic Lindsay Johnston in an essay from 2005. But more than the form of the structure itself, it is all the things you cannot see that defines the work of the best Australian architects.

"The river is the sea's dreaming," said Uncle Max, as if it made sense. Dreaming? To a western mind, the sentence is only barely graspable, and then only in a vague metaphorical or poetic sense, where one can imagine a river longing for the sea, or something like that. But Uncle Max makes it a statement, as if that was it, as if it were fact. So to him, it obviously is fact. Here, then, right next to us, is a reality in which there are not only dreams but dreamings, where the landscape is crisscrossed by songlines, where spirits speak to us, where trees need to be asked nicely before lending themselves to whatever enterprise you had in mind, be it bark canoe or building. What reality is that? Can we enter it, coming from somewhere altogether different? Can we live it?

Of course we can. Our bodies give us access to it all. We can walk the same paths, hearing the same dry leaves crunching underfoot; we can feel the same weight of rock and see the same river twisting between hill and meadow. And then, of course, there is architecture. The marvel of architecture is its endurance, which makes it available to us over time, which means that in time we can share the realities that it makes. Architecture takes material and places it in our way, and suddenly new realities are just there, occurring as we move, as we live and breathe, and what we never even thought to exist becomes fact. When we touch it, it is; just as it is only when we touch each other that we can be really sure we are alive, that we are here.

And with each thing our bodies touch, our stories grow. A building is not an object, never just a finite structure. It takes many different drawings to describe it. It takes many different people to construct it, each of them doing different things, and remembering and describing it differently afterwards – the plumber's house is not the same as the roofer's house or as the engineer's house. And afterwards, for each of us, the house is just another part of what we remember. Our story started before we arrived here and will continue afterwards. And so of course, the bloodlines of this architecture, these shifting and moving houses, flows from many sources, through the thin threads of association, of influence, of experience and understanding that connect all the people that have contributed to an understanding of this continent, this world, whatever their origins. And on a few, rare occasions, this understanding finds a durable physical expression in built form: an occasion where, finally, it dawns on us that different realities can indeed meet.

—

Ingerid Helsing Almaas

The fragile 'scaffold' like frame of the Israel House at Paradise Beach, NSW, built in 1992.

Bushland, Shoalhaven, NSW south coast.

Peter Stutchbury

Underpinnings

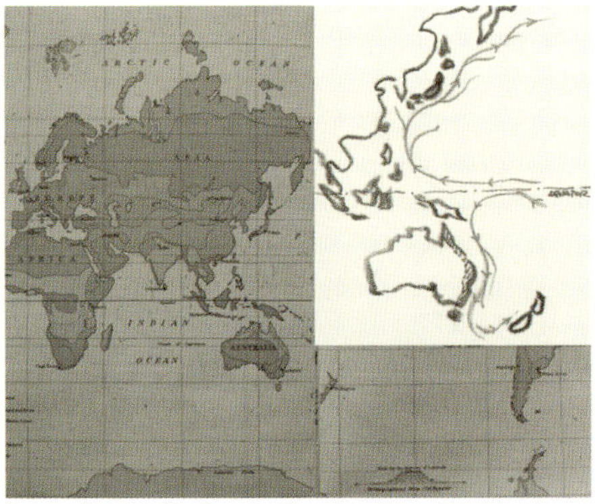

Australia is an isolated island. The east coast is fundamentally influenced by the Pacific Ocean with warm currents from the equator drifting both north and south. There is a Pacific nature that exists within traditional building stock, one of lightweight openness. This map indicates the isolation of Australia, its independence and the freedom that exists with this global location. In many ways this freedom surfaces within the creative arts.

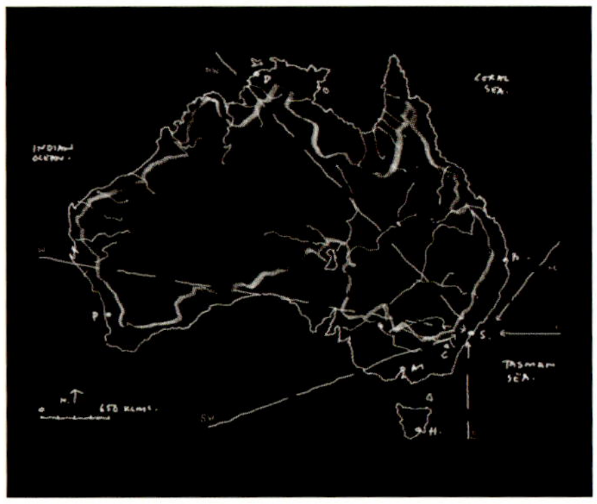

Essentially Australia is desert with a perimeter of river drained fertile land. Lake Eyre in upper South Australia is the sump for water caught inland and as depicted in the 2011 Queensland and Victorian floods, the massive movement of water informs much of the landscape. The arrows in this drawing indicate the direction of wind; the topography over which the wind travels has a legible influence on the nature of that wind – its velocity, moisture content and temperature.

Indigenous Australia is an assembly of many small countries within the overall landmass. Size of country generally reflects the amount of land necessary to support tribe and also to a lesser extent the type of topography. This map is fundamentally more sensible than the European subdivision, and immediately communicates the 'nature' of the country – wealth in this instance is survival not money.

A dawn shot at Uluru in the south west of the Northern Territory, 440km from Alice Springs. The landscape here is old and rhythmic. It is worn, tired and fragile and visually communicates eons of formation by water and wind. This is an ancient land.

A study in detail of the composition of our landscape reveals the repetitive patterns and marks of sand, stone, native grass and trees. There is an overall strength and beauty in the way those elements repeat and change in direct response to the composition to the climatic and geological conditions. The landscape can be traced and interpreted through its patterns.

With over 60,000 continuous years of habitation, Indigenous Australians understand the patterns that compose the land. Their art is repetitive, sensuous and interpretive. Generally works are painted in plan and express the nature of objects and place rather than the view as seen and expressed by the artist. This work by Willy Chungari is a painting depicting a section of his country.

I have been struggling to draw with originality for many years. Drawings have been a slave to the detail, which has been good for technique but not enjoyable. Several years ago I was forced to record a series of vignettes in the landscape quickly… my pen did not leave the paper and the resultant drawings, whilst not expected, were honest and interpretive. I enjoyed the process and no longer felt managed by my pencil. Finding this freedom has been a revelation.

The traditional European painting style is unlike the Indigenous way of seeing. We Europeans record a scene generally in elevation using colour, shading and composition to give value to the work. Often as a good artist grows, their work becomes more abstract but the perspective still remains in elevation. This way of observing is not as connected as someone who reads and represents the landscape… such as Indigenous Australians.

Young children retain a 'free mind', they can represent their dreams without the imposed overlay of school education, often their drawings are foreign and unique, representing the way they see their world. Slowly from the age of 7 onwards their art becomes more predictable. What are the influences that shift the mind from open to closed?

10 The Nation

Life takes flight from the salt of the earth

The patterns of Australia have legible historic logic. This country has the highest percent (except Antarctica) of original ancient landscape in existence (40%) largely due to the inhospitable nature of inland country. This newspaper article shows Lake Eyre in flood after being dry for over a decade. Within 24 hours the pelicans are flying in from the coast thousand of kilometres away, marine life that has lain dormant suddenly becomes active. We call this 'embedded knowledge'. This country does not experience four seasons but a variety of changes, some repetitive some infrequent over the decades, over the centuries.

Fire is part of the psyche of this country. It has developed as part of the evolution of the place. A large dry continent, with spectacular thunder and lightning storms brings fire. Indigenous Australians used fire to assist in food gathering. Much flora has adapted to the devastation of fire – surviving and regenerating within weeks. Australia is familiar to fire, to Europeans it is foreign. Fire is one of the natures of this land.

Approximately 90% of Australians live within 100km of the coast. We are a nation with an orientation around water. Water recreation, water as a resource, water as a definitive perimeter of our continent. As a consequence of where we settle, light reflected off water is also part of our knowledge. This is bright and blue and powerful – learning to consider this light informs our architecture.

On a 2010 trip to the semi-arid 100,000-acre property of my mother's family, I saw this specific sky, I asked my cousin what it meant and he answered, 'about 10mm of rain about 12am tonight'. There was 7mm of rain and it fell at about 1am. The sky is a barometer of the day and beyond. Sailors, farmers and surfers understand these patterns – but for too many it has been lost.

The ground is a different register. It reflects activity and type. It can indicate geology through plant type, even land fertility. Topography talks of water flow and ground configurations that reveal lines in the land that are sacred and that should be respected. Indigenous Australians refer to earth as mother, that is why they pay it such respect, it is important we begin to respect the value of mother earth.

One can become accustomed to reading the landscape; the patterns that allow us to translate history, composition change and context. The land comes alive with clues and explanations, rarely does clarity not exist, we only need to look, wonder and find. This scene is in the Kimberleys in northwest Western Australia. Obviously this is a riverbed where water flows in large volumes and quickly, the lean of the trees indicates direction of flow and debris in branches height of river. If we study the detail, we can determine the origin of the debris and therefore the source.

Landscape has structure. Here a wonderful rock ledge is simply supported by the corbelling layers of rock that step out to the very edge. This allows for a majestic cantilever. Often clues to structure drawn from nature, at both a macro and micro level, can be directly translated into architectural expression.

This detail explains further. Here are two images of moss, both on the same parcel of land. The first indicating time without rain, one can test the dryness of the moss manually and estimate land condition. Also this moss will only occur in low-lying water catchment areas and normally where the water sits. Detail two shows moss (and lichen) after rain; possibly within one week and definitely not in summer; but significantly the moss grows on the southern side of the tree – a compass.

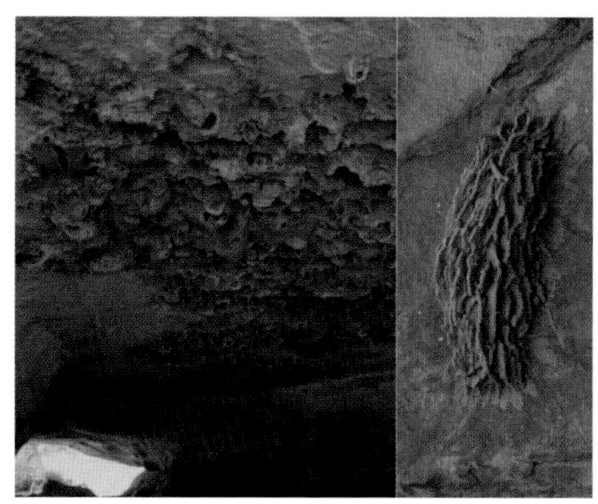

Our birds, insects, animals and fish all have adapted to place. Here mud swallows nesting on the leeward side of a cave benefit from the windward breeze, they are also cooled by the thermal mass of the rock, which is 7°C cooler than the surrounding environment. This serrated mud wasp nest (note, mud from different area) is designed to effectively disperse heat. The larger the surface area of the nest the more the prevailing breeze cools it. Nests are strategically positioned to catch the breeze.

The crocodile dates back about 200 million years. According to Darwinism the animals most likely to flourish are those that are best able to adapt to their environment – 'survival of the fittest'. There are several aspects of the crocodile that fascinate me; being a cold-blooded reptile the modules on the back increase the surface area to facilitate heat gain.

The European sheep never originated or evolved in this country so had no adaptations to manage heat, lack of water or a diet of less nutritious native grass. Sheep are not used to travelling long distances, while their cloven hoofs tear and compress the fragile landscape. Similarly houses that have not adapted to their environment struggle to survive.

Our childhood provides fundamental guidance towards the construction of our thinking. Our inherited ways are tested and new ways explored. Overall life is a composition. Many of my formative experiences were on the family property near Cobar, a semi-arid 100,000-acre parcel of land 750km west of Sydney. The homestead was constructed by my uncle from recycled army huts. The house compound was self-sufficient and completely off the grid. The value of water was learnt at an early age and distance from town put added value on how resources were managed.

My father's family going back several generations were builders. My father was an engineer, his company was the head contractor for the construction of power stations. He had an eye for detail, low maintenance and practicality. We would work alongside him in the garage as he built billy carts, restored lawn mowers, made tools, made a sailing dingy, cubby houses and more, we learnt to be makers.

Summer holidays were spent on Pittwater, north of Sydney living in a small holiday cottage that opened directly onto the beach. We learnt to sail, surf, swim, fish and explore. Holidays there were filled with fantasy.

Growing up in Australia often involves travel and camping. This informality suits both the climate and the nature of place. It was common to chase waves up and down the coast as a surfer, to throw some gear in the wagon, just water and cooking equipment and then to sleep in the landscape with the stars as ceiling. This nomadic lifestyle permeates the youth and becomes part of the Australian psyche. That is until luxury and convenience becomes more dominant for some.

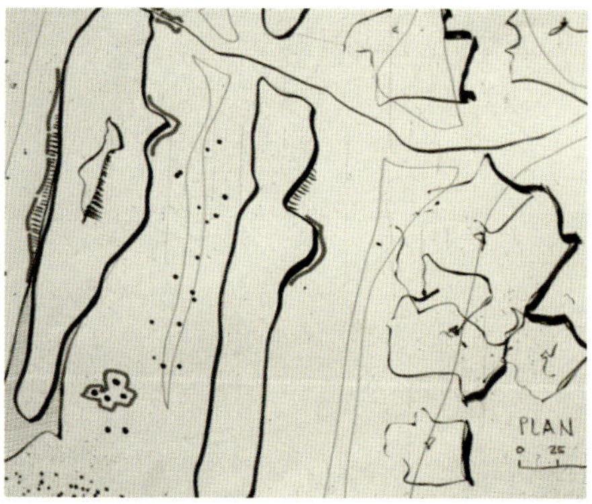

The traditional Indigenous Australian house is landscape. It is usually temporarily occupied and located near a water source. Invariably there is some shelter but essentially it is rooms in the landscape for cooking, talking, making, sleeping. Privacy is not a priority. As the room is big what is fundamental is sharing – it is not a place for selfish behavior.

One element of permanence may be a cave. Roof, wall, fire, a place of human security, a place for the elders. There is an element of respect that comes with the strength of this room as it occupies a transparent forest. One can imagine story telling here with flickering firelight reflecting against the roof. A dry warm earth floor and prospect, the essential elements.

Two impermanent Indigenous Australian dwellings. On the left a possum skin dome hut from the southern state of Victoria, with its small opening to secure against the cold. On the right an elevated hut responds to the tropical heat of the Northern Territory. Constructed with a single bark skin roof, a similar method used for canoe making, the elevation lifts residents away from crocodiles, smoke from the fire below deters mosquitoes.

I stumbled upon this settlement on the south coast of New South Wales. An 84-year-old gentleman had lived there 15 years. It consisted of a roof shelter with a perimeter seat. He used this space for cooking and living. Alongside was a caravan bedroom and secure store on rubber wheels. He pushed the trailer into the sun in winter and back under the shade in summer. He farmed the land.

One of my favorite homes is this small complex on the Darling River, which flows from north to south across outback Queensland and New South Wales. The complex has a social room with fireplace and adjustable orange plastic awning. There are two adjacent sleeping tents and ablutions out the back away from the living environment. In many ways this is a clear diagram for a lifestyle strategy.

Early Australian beach and country houses were small, practical, sensible and sustainable. Up to 15 people would occupy buildings during peak times and the freedom of the cottage was often reflected by the manner of those who occupied. The minimal footprint and the use of low embodied energy materials along with sensible planning and eternal living zones was a good model. Somewhere somehow it got lost.

The 'Pacific nature' in buildings is found throughout the Pacific all the way up to Japan. Traditionally the Japanese built lightweight, small, restrained, ordered, recyclable and operable houses. Generally with thick roofs to manage temperature variation and lightweight walls, creating airlocks and also connecting with landscape. The traditional Pacific age old model made significant sense.

Here on the Myall lakes on the central coast of New South Wales the pews for the 'Church in the Forest' are made from the trees cut from the footprint. This beautiful room is a re-interpreted forest. It is suitable, explanatory and connected. An economical place of human gathering.

Semi open-air picture theatres were common occurrence in the 1970's. Canvas slung between a continuous top and bottom rail - beautiful and sensible for our climate. The retreat of the covered zone used when required. This form of theatre reflects our ability to make any event a social interaction. A fun and economical structure adapted easily to performance.

Semi-open surf pavilions were also commonplace during the 1970's. It was a delight to arrive back from the surf to shower and dress in the sun or shade as desired. These buildings were easy to manage; their function reinforced their recreational nature. Councils decided to roof the open areas, as they were concerned people would get wet if it rained. This put an end to an element of fun.

Citizens have allowed property developers to define the nature of home. It has become more important to own a home than to consider its impact. Australians have fallen prey to the ownership frenzy of the quarter acre block. Lessons and references of the past have been lost to an economic quick fix. It is no surprise that architect-designed homes, those that are designed to nurture, have significantly longer lives.

The introduction of lifts and air conditioning means that we could pack people into vertical boxes - a property developers dream. Small land area, maximum persons, total repetition, irrelevant orientation, elimination of natural systems. These units serve a narrow purpose and have changed the very nature of settlement.

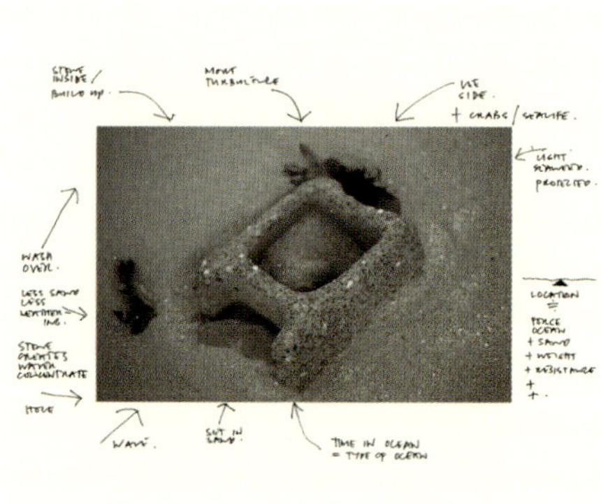

This man made block of masonry found at the edge of the ocean communicates both history and a response to place. Its response is logical and unique; a steel block would be different. Our homes need to understand and reflect where they are; this is not a chore but simply a balance of legible considerations, as we learn to occupy our landscape with a local understanding we begin to be responsible.

Our elders are those who have travelled long distances and gathered wisdom, we should orientate ourselves around those who are most important to our path, yet also pay respect to all who have taken the time to evolve. Lessons need to be comprehended and passed on so that traditional and acquired wisdom is not lost to bright lights and fast cars. The single word that explains this process is respect.
Left: Uncle Max Dulumunmun Harrison
Right: Richard Leplastrier

The computer is a tool but its fascination and ease have allowed it to become entertainment. If you want to learn about crocodiles you can, or water, drawing, fires, weather, moss, painting, sheep, Pacific Ocean buildings, mud nests, camping, sun, shade, Japan and elders. We need to become aware of how we gather information. There is a remarkable difference between googling camping and physically smelling the smoke and watching the flame of the campfire. We must be careful not to eliminate the tactility of experience and eye, brain, body co-ordination response. Try hugging a computer.

Effective communication is a primary tool within the practice of architecture. As we begin a project it is important that those making the work are informed. This information at its most elemental can be design intent, at its more complex can be design philosophy. It is fundamental to acknowledge the contribution that a team of persons makes toward a final project. The human touch invariably gives the work humanity.

Peter Stutchbury at Glenn Murcutt's 'master work', the Arthur and Yvonne Boyd Art Centre, Riversdale.

Peter Stutchbury Architecture
Projects in Brief

North Durras, NSW, 2011

Israel House

1986 — 1992, Paradise Beach, NSW, Australia

This house sits on a difficult site: steep, westward facing, damp and cold in winter. The building is placed away from the road below a rock ledge amongst the forest, yet reaching high enough to catch available sun. Three distinct functions are provided.

Downstairs is private, made of intimate ground and cave-related wet rooms. The mid level is a social room, highlighting the rock face and the extensive waters of the bay. The upper level is an isolated, sun-drenched room that encompasses the entire site. A large protective roof caps the whole building. Phillip Drew says this is "architecture conceived in much the same way as a piece of furniture, such is the craft and care of assembly."

Location: Paradise Beach, Northern Beaches, NSW Design: 1986 Construction: 1992 Architects: Peter Stutchbury Builders: Peter Stutchbury, Ken Israel, Jeff Broadfield

Richardson Faculty, Nurses Wing at Newcastle University with EJE
1992 — 1995, University of Newcastle, NSW, Australia

The Nurses' Faculty applies advanced environmental and energy saving design. A geothermal field producing 21°C - reticulated water enables a 450-seat auditorium to be naturally air-conditioned. Air temperature is moderated by human heat in winter, producing an optimal 24°C in the auditorium. The building was the earliest buildings in Australia to integrate a geothermal field for air conditioning on this scale. The building links two existing structures and has little impact upon the surrounding woodland. The building is sited to retain the forest, rainwater is collected in retention ponds for irrigation.

Location: University of Newcastle, Newcastle, NSW Design: 1992 Construction: 1995 Architects: Peter Stutchbury, Doug White (EJE), Fergus Scott, Grant Mears, Geoff Whitnall (EJE), Debra McKendry-Hunt (EJE) Landscape Architect: Phoebe Pape

Sydney International Archery Centre
1996 — 1999, Homebush, NSW, Australia

A large awning roof twists across the northern boundary of the shooting field of the Olympic Archery Pavilion, reflecting the dynamic yet mathematic nature of the sport. A combination of light and heavy structure, the building offers an endless verandah. The roof is the subtle protector, changing the scale and providing extensive cover to the rooms beneath as it twists down against the western weather end. This separate "fly" roof reduces maintenance, provides shade and allows for a column free shooting zone, while reflecting light onto building modules below. Disconnected from the roof, these sheltered modules can be moved. On a site of potential subsidence, building flexibility provides for long term functional use.

Location: Homebush, Sydney, NSW Design: 1996 – 1998 Construction: 1999 Architects: Peter Stutchbury, Ray Fitzgibbon, Fergus Scott, Katrina Julienne Engineers: Robert Herbertson Landscape Architect: Phoebe Pape Builder: Cooinda Construction

Bay House
1996 — 2000, Watsons Bay, NSW, Australia

The opportunity to design in the company of lucid and informed clients is one of architecture's great pleasures. This building exemplifies the curiosity and intelligence of several people. Located within an urban precinct, but with special outlets to landscape and harbour, this project demanded discipline. Bay House is informed by 'T' walls in plan where you can always find sun, shade or shelter. The building is a simple translation of room and opportunity – simple plan, a subtle section. The house considers an old watercourse, the light off the water and ultimately how one might make a camp by the harbour. Bay House is a big boat shed that marries the latest technologies with the age-old qualities of a retreat and dwelling.

Location: Watsons Bay, Sydney, NSW Design: 1996 – 2000 Construction: 1998 – 2002 Architects: Peter Stutchbury, James Stockwell Engineers: Professor Max Irvine Landscape Architect: Phoebe Pape Builder: Barradean Pty Ltd

Birabahn with Richard Leplastrier and Sue Harper

1996 — 2002, University of Newcastle, NSW, Australia

The competition-winning design for the Aboriginal and Torres Strait Islander Multipurpose Centre evolved significantly to embrace the practical requirements of the end users. The building has become representative of Indigenous cultural aspirations: it represents future values alongside traditional means. Many visitors remark on the emotional 'warmth' of the building. The design was informed by computer modelling for thermal performance, natural light and ventilation and achieves remarkable comfort levels most days of the year without any air conditioning. Birabahn goes beyond conventional buildings – it demonstrates the remarkable synergies that can arise when goodwill and cultural understanding are applied in a real way to reconciliation.

Location: University of Newcastle, Newcastle, NSW Design: 1996 -1997 Construction: 1998 - 2002 Architects: Peter Stutchbury, Sue Harper, Richard Leplastrier, Shane Blue, Richard Smith Engineers: Professor Max Irvine, Northrops Pty Ltd Landscape: Mim Woodland & Philip Pollard Builder: Stronach

Life Sciences Link Building with Suters Architects

1997 — 2001, University of Newcastle, NSW, Australia

The Life Sciences Project is a complex research and laboratory-based building that assimilates the research requirements of both Biology and Medicine. PSA and Suters Architects were awarded this project through competition, primarily because the design maintains service flexibility, solves numerous public access problems, compliments adjoining buildings and maintains a "lightness" of building on campus. Significantly, the building was at the time one of the largest precast cantilevers of its type internationally. The north-facing facade enables light to penetrate deep into the public zones. The building integrates its neighbours with precision, while a central public zone created by the grid of the colonnade creates a central piazza.

Location: University of Newcastle, Newcastle, NSW Design: 1997 Construction: 1999 - 2001 Architects: Peter Stutchbury, Fergus Scott, James Stockwell, Brian Suters, James Fraser, Dino DiPaolo, Chris McBriarty, Graham Tumpane, Daniel Arzamendia, Matthew Markham-Lee Engineers: Professor Max Irvine, Neil Petherbridge, Northrops Pty Ltd Builder: Laheys Construction Pty Ltd

Reeves House with Sue Harper
1997 — 1999, Clareville, NSW, Australia

The Reeves House, designed in association with Sue Harper is essentially a large living room, an open space for sleeping and cooking made from two blade walls placed in the landscape. The north of the main blade is the zone of human interaction – the sunny and lively side. Between the blades is a subdued and subtle gallery zone, here light reflects through a clear screen above. The roof floats above the living spaces and twists through the landscape, lifting to the morning sun and dropping over the western deck and afternoon sun. The kitchen is the focal point, stretching from inside to outside. Thermal mass is used for controlling heating and cooling. A concrete floor, and concrete blade walls heat up during winter days and radiate heat at night. In summer they maintain a constant low heat.

Location: Clareville, Northern Beaches, NSW Design: 1997 Construction: 1998 - 1999 Architects: Peter Stutchbury, Sue Harper Engineers: Eva Tihanyi Landscape Architect: Phoebe Pape Builder: Craig Pocklington

Springwater
1998 — 2005, Seaforth, NSW, Australia

Springwater is located on a steep west facing Sydney Harbour foreshore dotted with sandstone boulders and Angophora trees. The site offers an outlook, through foliage, to the sky and the water. Conceived as a camp, the house frame is concrete onto stone with long concrete columns marching down the site. A series of house platforms with operable facades allow the building to be directed by its occupants, acting as an open shelter in the bush, or as a series of secure rooms. Long simply framed spaces characterise all three levels of the building. The sturdy frame is lightened by revealing the structure, while lighting, joinery and fixtures are all considered as intimate elements of the building, these exposed fixtures and raw finishes are intended as the only devices to soften a tough structure.

Location: Seaforth, Northern Beaches, NSW Design: 1998 - 2000 Construction: 2001 - 2003 Architects: Peter Stutchbury, James Stockwell Engineers: Professor Max Irvine Landscape Architect: Phoebe Pape Builder: David Watson, Watpow Constructions

Bangalay
2000 — 2005, Upper Kangaroo Valley, NSW, Australia

Bangalay's greatest attribute is its connection with the land. The site, once part of the Buderoo National Park on the South Coast of New South Wales, is a large clearing with a dam to the north. The house is an elegant shed orientated towards the north for passive solar gain. Circulation runs from an offset corridor. The roof rises toward the east, where the living areas are located, providing a generous sense of space. The heart of the house is a large sheltered courtyard, which serves as a mediator between the public and private spaces. Large timber framed sliding glass doors surround the house, allowing the building to open and close and frame the landscape it so comfortably sits within. A large cantilevered verandah roof hangs above these openings, providing shelter to the living areas below.

Location: Upper Kangaroo Valley, Southern Highlands, NSW Design: 2000 Construction: 2001 - 2005 Architects: Peter Stutchbury, Marika Jarv Engineers: Professor Max Irvine Landscape Architect: Phoebe Pape Builder: Tony Lake Constructions

Cardboard House with the Ian Buchan Fell Housing Research Unit
For House of the Future Exhibition, 2004

This prototype house explores the humble but versatile materiality of cardboard. In keeping with the low fidelity nature of the material, the design avoids complex construction and technology, focusing on non-toxic, expandable, lightweight ideas that can be simply assembled. The building began as a frame based on packaging technology for wine bottles. Other elements are integrated with the minimum of fixings, relying on simple interlocking parts. The volume is a simple living space – service pods (kitchen & bathroom) are relocatable in the building or under the verandah. The house can expand with additions such as windows, verandahs, bedroom modules, shelving and furniture. With a basic scaffold, this house can be hand assembled, simply by slotting the elements together, by two people in six hours.

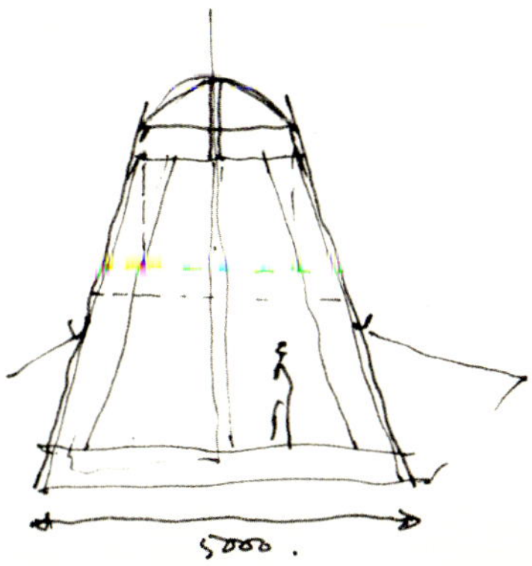

Design: 2004 Construction: 2004 Architects: Peter Stutchbury, Richard Smith, Matt Markham-Lee Project Team: PSA office Col James, Adriano Pupilli, Eboni James, Hugo Monline, Mat Lipson, Caroline Comino, Brendon Miller Engineers: Professor Max Irvine, Dr David Gunaratnam Builders: Visy Industries, PSA and Multiplex Images: John Gollings

SCU Innovation Centre
1st National Design Competition
2001, Lismore, NSW, Australia

Situated a few kilometres south east of Lismore, on the North Coast of New South Wales, Innovation Centre is an unbuilt concept for an international centre for research, development and commercial production on natural plant products and is intended to be a sustainable and innovative workplace. This project represents a unique opportunity for a building design to divert the servicing and finish values entrenched in larger building works. The building is orientated west of north, using the fall of land to advantage – other than a minor cut of 500mm, the existing contours are maintained. A physical corridor is laid over the building footprint allowing the majority of building users access to a significant fig tree on the site. The long western verandah is a deliberate visual reference to local building typologies. This building integrates environmental systems into the live workings of the building aesthetics.

Location: Southern Cross University, Lismore, north coast, NSW Competition: 2000 Design: 2001 - 2002 Architects: Peter Stutchbury, Sacha Zehnder, Richard Smith Engineers: Professor Max Irvine

Learning Commons
1st National Design Competition
2005 — 2006, Albury, NSW, Australia

The Learning Commons is an unbuilt concept for a new kind of library that balances aesthetic, functional and environmental considerations. A trombe wall forms the entire northern Facade of the building. Solar heat falling onto the surface is harnessed and utilised rather than penetrating into the interior.

The northern face of the wall is clad in rusting steel, keeping summer heat off the thermal mass in the corridor. The height of the northern corridor and outlets along the ridge provide natural venting. Air is drawn from the southern occupied zone into the corridor and rises out into the atmosphere. A glazed roof on the corridor intensifies the draw-through of hot air; shading provides control for different seasons. Fresh air replenishes the southern spaces via a large earth pipe with an intake located in the shaded bush to the south of the building.

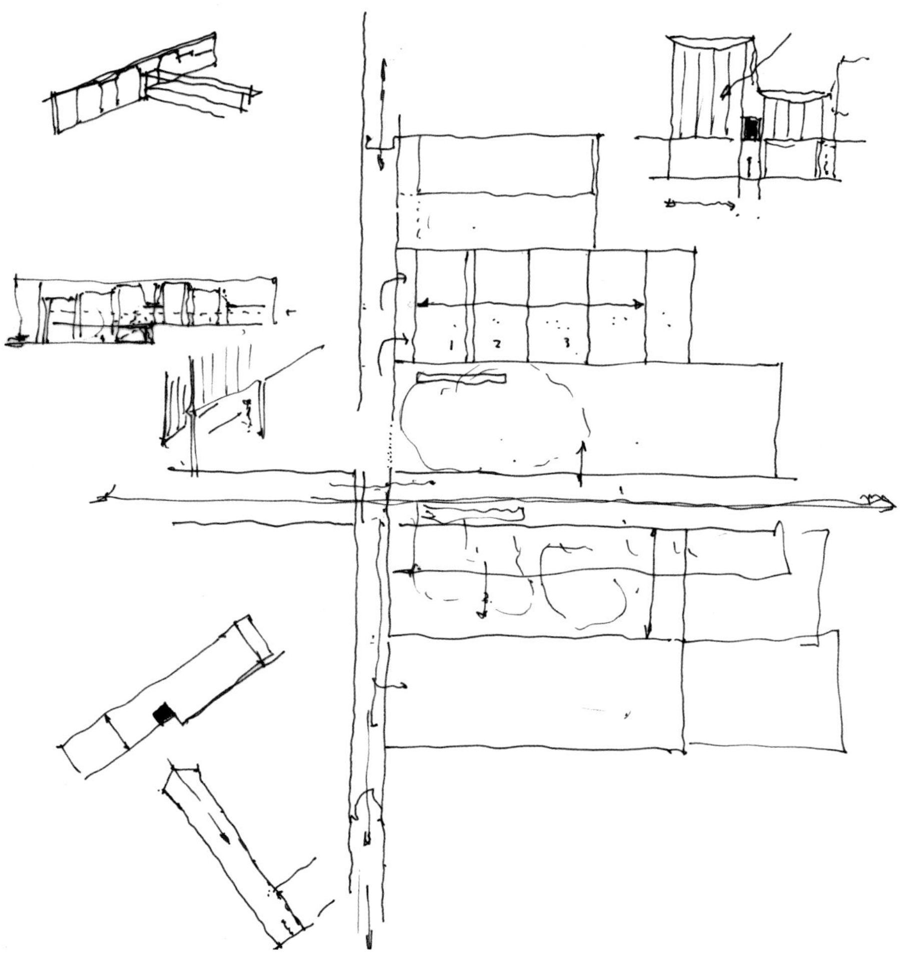

Location: Charles Sturt University, Thurgoona Campus, Albury, NSW Competition: 2005 Design: 2006 Construction stopped: May 2007 Architects: PSA office, Richard Smith, Ulrika Saar Engineers: Professor Max Irvine, Steensen Varming Managing Contractor: ZAUNER Constructions

Torovo House

1st International Living Steel Competition
2008

The Living Steel International Extreme Housing Competition asked for a sustainable steel house for Cherepovets, Russia a city that experiences -48°C temperatures. The traditional buildings of northern Scandinavia and Russia were studied along with the principles of Igloo construction. The qualities of steel were re-considered along with existing technology used in Australia to resist heat. Every aspect of the solution in this case considers how to retain heat energy produced by operation of the house. Heat is trapped and moved to a collection point, where it is then redistributed through a storage wall. The wall is made of sheet steel filled with gravel and acts as a large thermal mass radiator. The project communicates the ability to adapt philosophy to places and problems outside of the traditional environment of the practice.

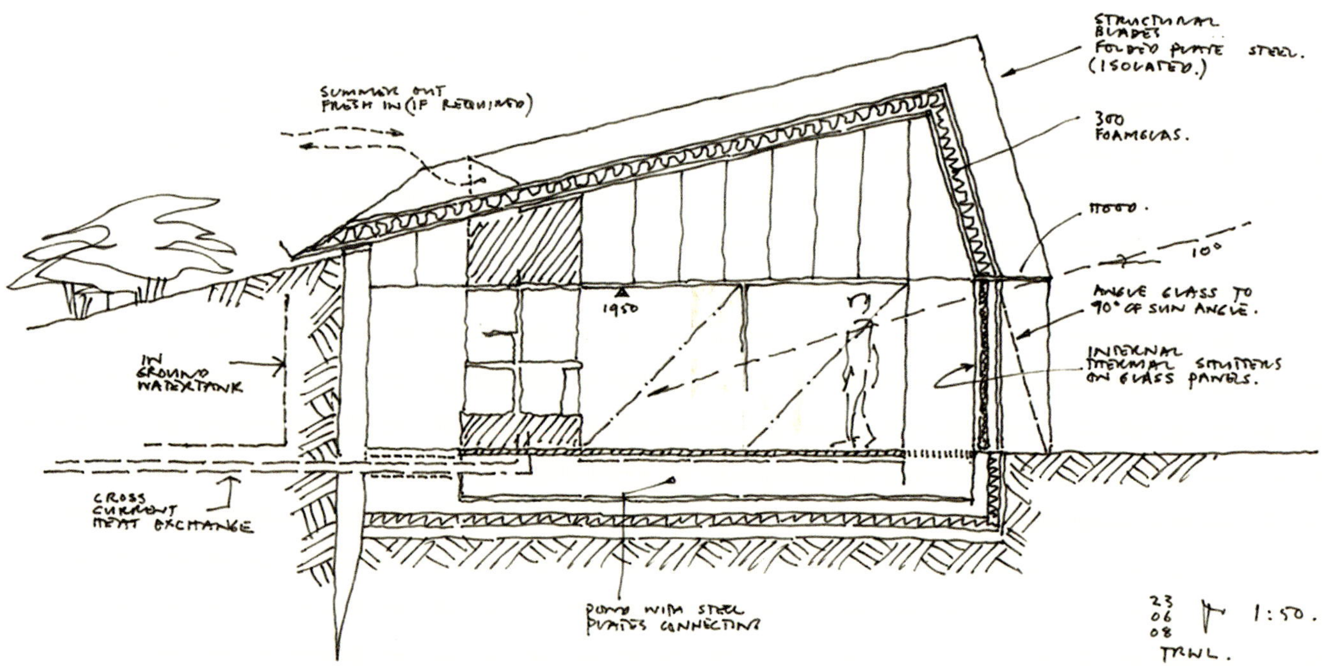

Location: Cherepovets, Russia
[illegible]
Construction: 2010 Architects:
Peter Stutchbury, PSA office, Richard Smith, Ann Bassett Engineers:
Professor Max Irvine

2000 — 2005

Wagga Wagga, NSW, Australia

Deepwater Woolshed

Location: Wagga Wagga, Riverina, NSW Elevation: 147m Prevailing winter wind: East Prevailing summer wind: East, northeast Min temperature: -8°C Max temperature: +44°C Annual precipitation: 778mm Design: 2001- 2003 Construction: 2003 - 2005 Architects: Peter Stutchbury, Sacha Zehnder Engineers: Professor Max Irvine Builder: Atlex Stockyards, Dubbo

Wool production has long been a mainstay of Australia's highly productive farming sector. The seasonal trade of sheep shearing is subsequently deeply rooted within Australian culture as famously demanding work for tough farming men, shearing sheep in the heat and dust of a sun soaked tin shed.

This woolshed project at Bulls Run property, north west of Wagga Wagga, 200km inland from the coast, in regional New South Wales, re-thinks the design of traditional woolsheds in order to create an optimal work environment for shearers, while also meeting the highest standards for wool preparation and sheep handling.

The extreme heat experienced during the shearing season drove the placement, orientation, form and materiality of this building. The efficient movement of the sheep in a low stress environment and the technical requirements of the process of shearing drove the planning and layout.

The building has embraced a range of design solutions to contend with the summer heat. Alongside optimal orientation to capture prevailing northeasterly breezes that cross ventilate the interior, overhangs of a large portal frame roof provide shade to the walls and provide undercover sheep storage and access. A reticulated irrigation system sprays cooling water onto the roof. Large expanded mesh screens have been hung to the southwest, providing protection from the prevailing wind. Cascading water across these suspended surfaces utilises the cross-ventilating breeze and evaporative cooling, lowering working temperatures.

Strip skylights provide natural lighting. The entire structure is bolted together; all linings, cladding and floors are screwed and fixed. Thus the entire shed is demountable. The usage of a structural roofing system was an iniative providing additional planning flexibility.

This project sets out to provide a quality work environment for one of Australia's oldest trades. The resulting building has elevated the task of shearing at Bulls Run, while reinterpreting the traditional built form of an Australian icon. This is a sophisticated passive building in tune with land, man and beast.

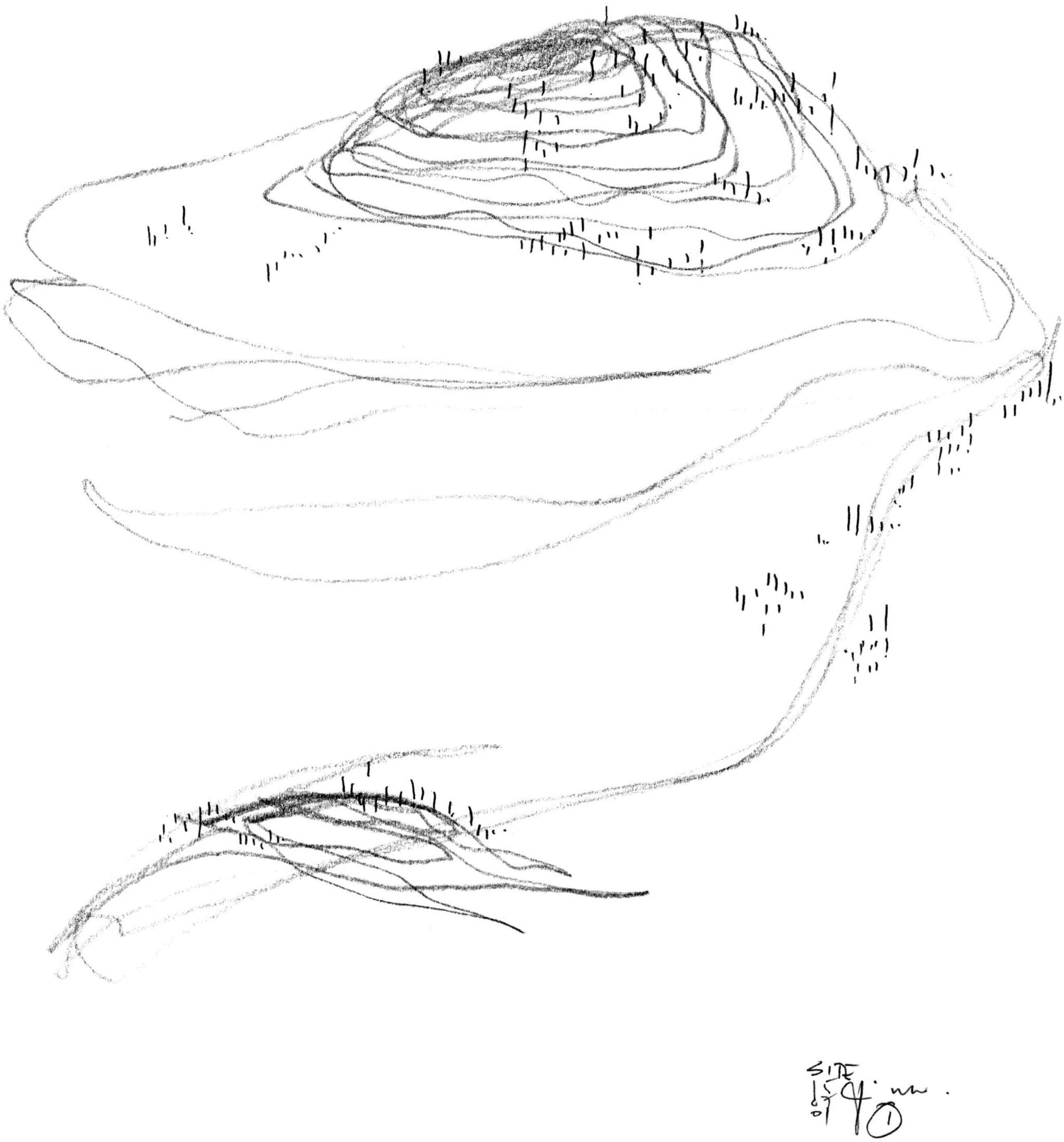

Birds eye view of site.

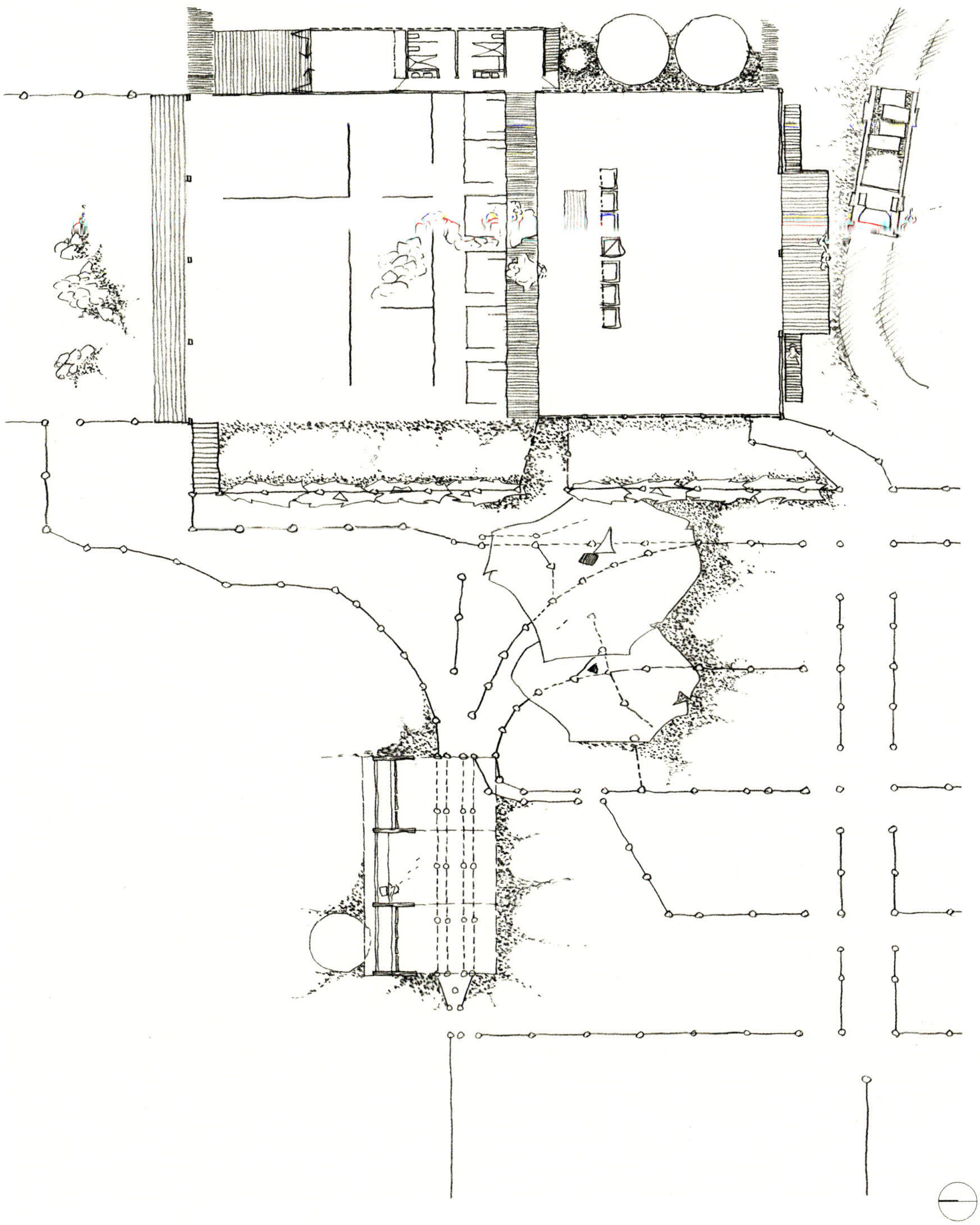

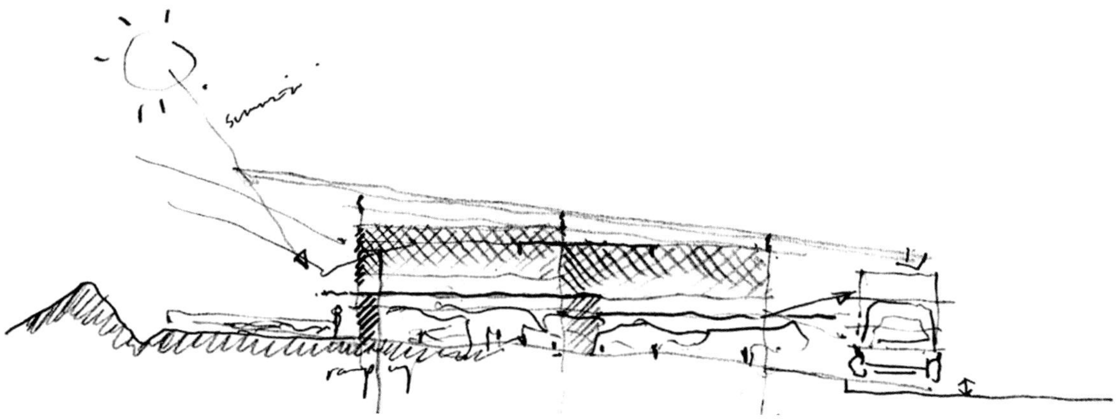

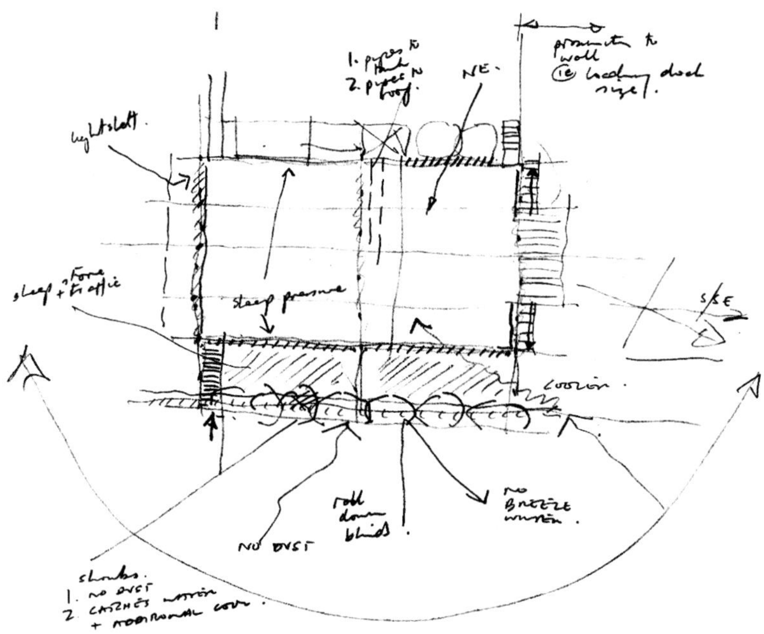
NE.
S/SE
roll down blinds.
NO DUST
NO BREEZE WINTER.

Top:
Depth of roof profile – roof as structure.

Bottom:
Shearers enjoying the 'resort' like shed facilities.

Previous page:
Simple portal frames with roof as structure, walls for light and ventilation.
This page:
An inclined plane, big overlap, light and shade, tuned to site.

Water dripping across the expanded mesh screen cools incoming air, which transfers through louvres into the shed. Stock can rest in the shade.

2000 — 2007
Tarago, NSW, Australia
Paddock House

This is a modern farmhouse in an outback paddock scattered with clusters of hardy eucalypts, a moment of shelter in a flat landscape stretching outwards. The weather here is dry, and the earth white. The ground is quickly nourished by infrequent rain, which momentarily transforms the landscape into a soft, grassy plain.

The family that dwells here breed Kashmir goats and harvest their fine wool. They adhere to sustainable farming practices to fit with the fragile ecosystem. The farmhouse nourishes and embraces their life as they work with the land and the animals.

Paddock House is a simple shelter, two strong masonry walls and two planes of roof that provide shelter and the comforts of a home. Thick walls that provide thermal mass to manage heating and cooling delineate the living and sleeping spaces. Joining these spaces is this walled mixed-use artery of storage, service and thoroughfare.

The roof is a large canopy that collects precious rainwater and shelters generous outdoor spaces, including a west-facing deck and an east-facing fly mesh room.

Construction is simple, straightforward and economical, compiled with quality of finish and longevity of performance in mind. In keeping with the agricultural nature of the building, key elements can easily be prefabricated and shipped to the site for quick assembly.

Responding to the landscape, this house is like a resting insect, with low demands for energy and water, generating warmth and coolness from the systems integral and inherent in the house, a place to retreat and replenish, while remaining of the land.

Location: Tarago, Southern Tablelands, NSW Elevation: 684m Prevailing winter wind: West Prevailing summer wind: West Min temperature: -10°C Max temperature: +41°C Annual precipitation: 517mm Design: 2000 Construction: 2004 – 2007 Architects: Peter Stutchbury, Sacha Zehnder Engineers: Professor Max Irvine Builder: Andy Pinkas

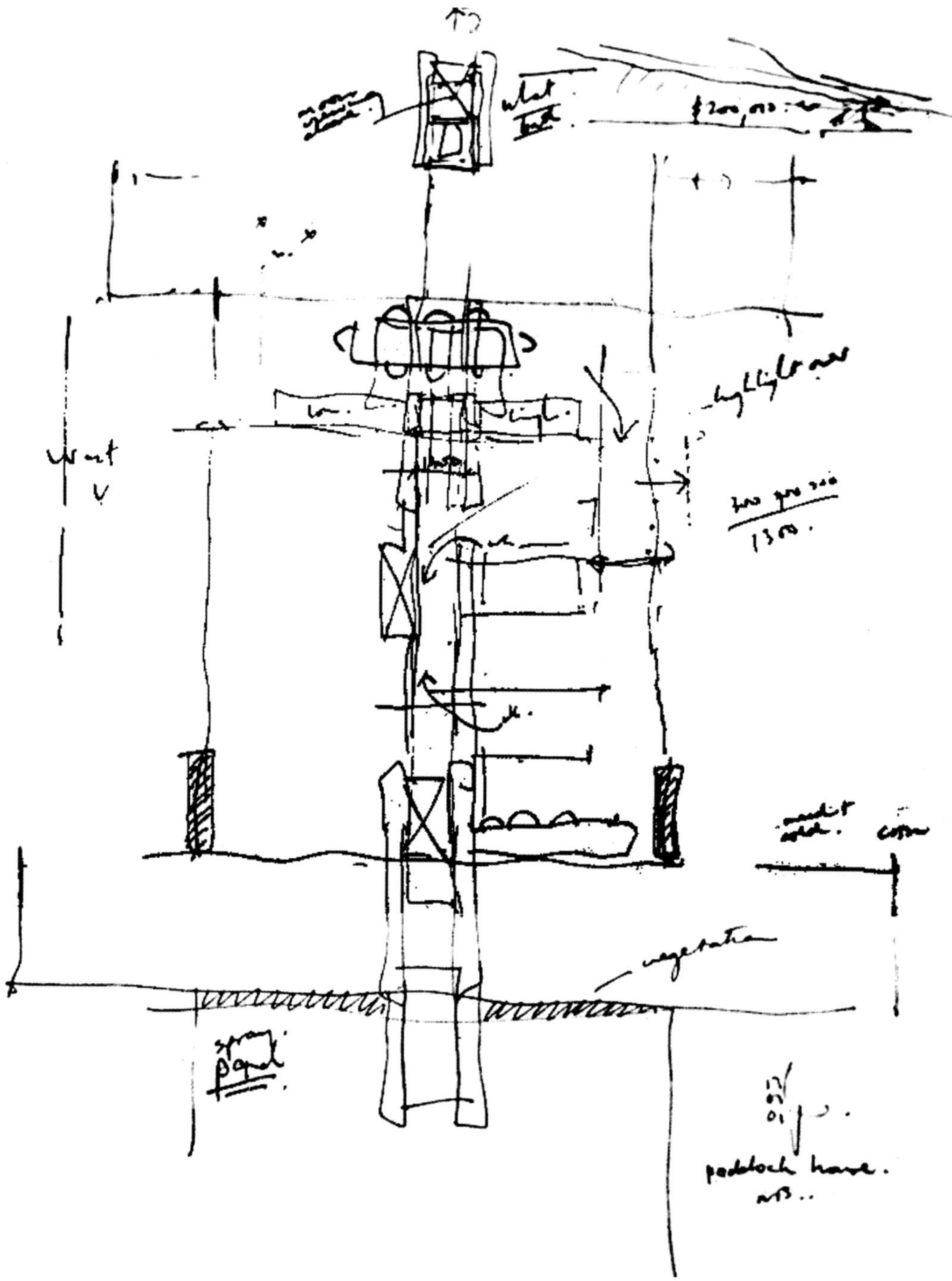

Concept plan.

This page top:
Entry avenue.
This page bottom:
Landscape integrates into house.

Next page:
Lightweight prefabricated steel frame adjacent to masonry core, verandahs integrate with the landscape.

This page:
Entry pond for reflection and evaporative cooling.

Next page:
Wrap around verandah with adjoining cooking area adjacent to shade tree.

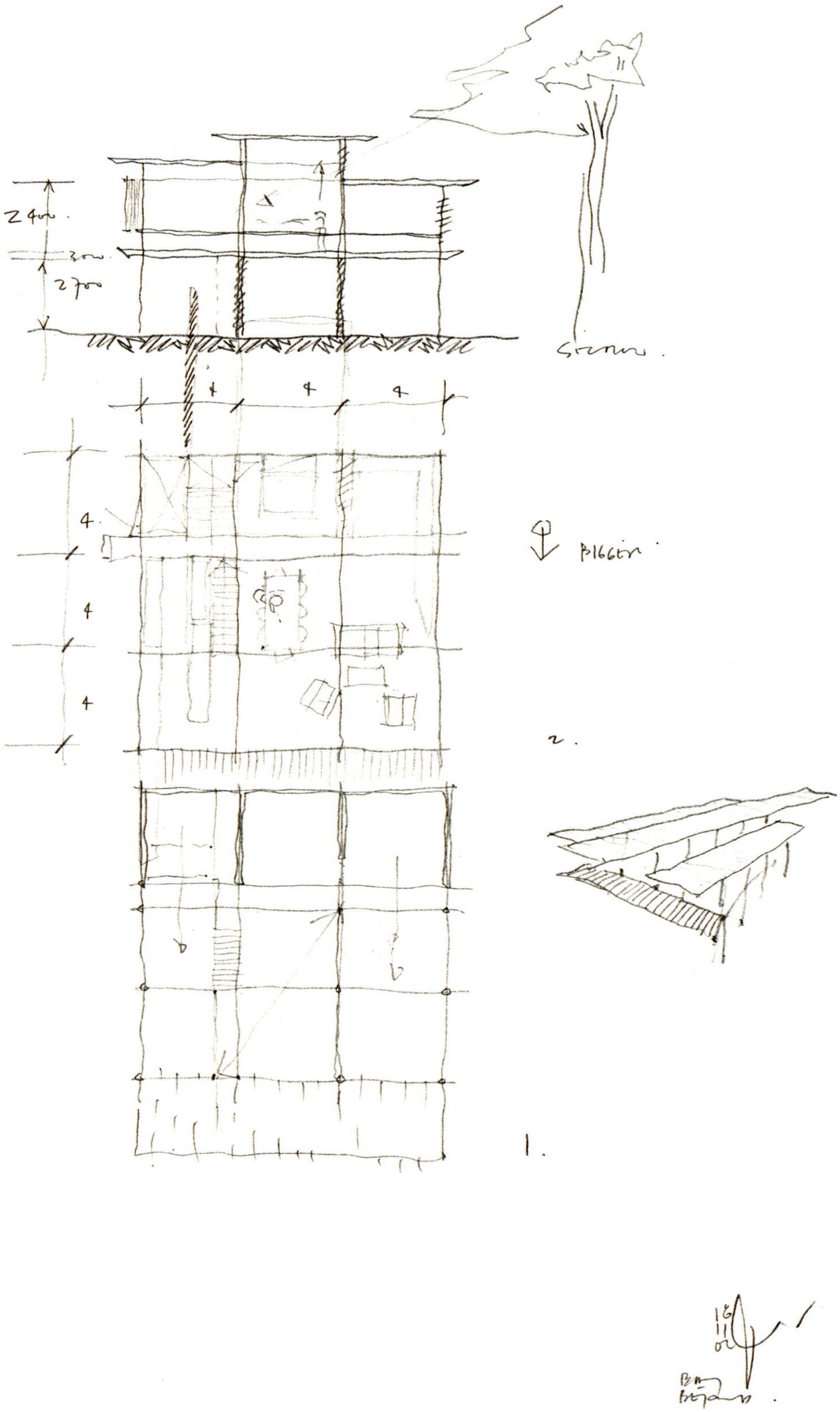
2400.
2700
4
4
4
4
4
4
2.
1.

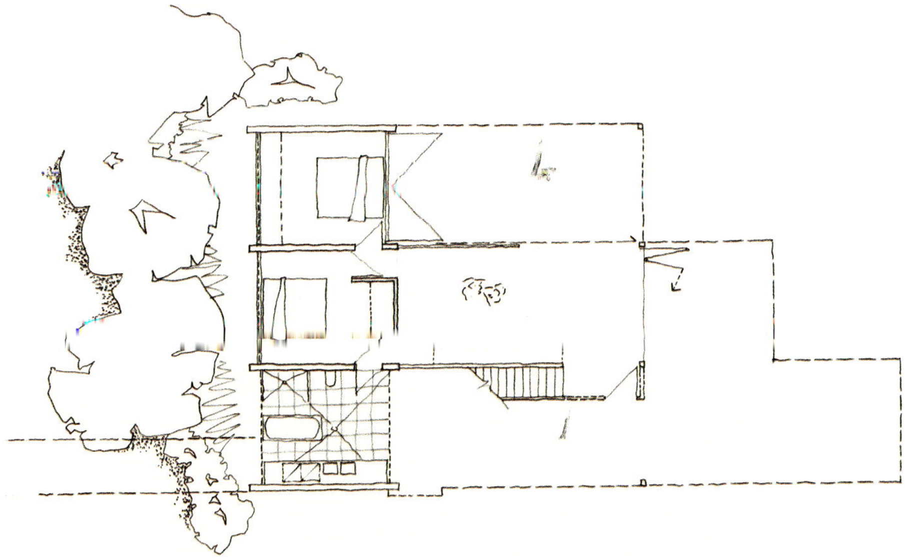

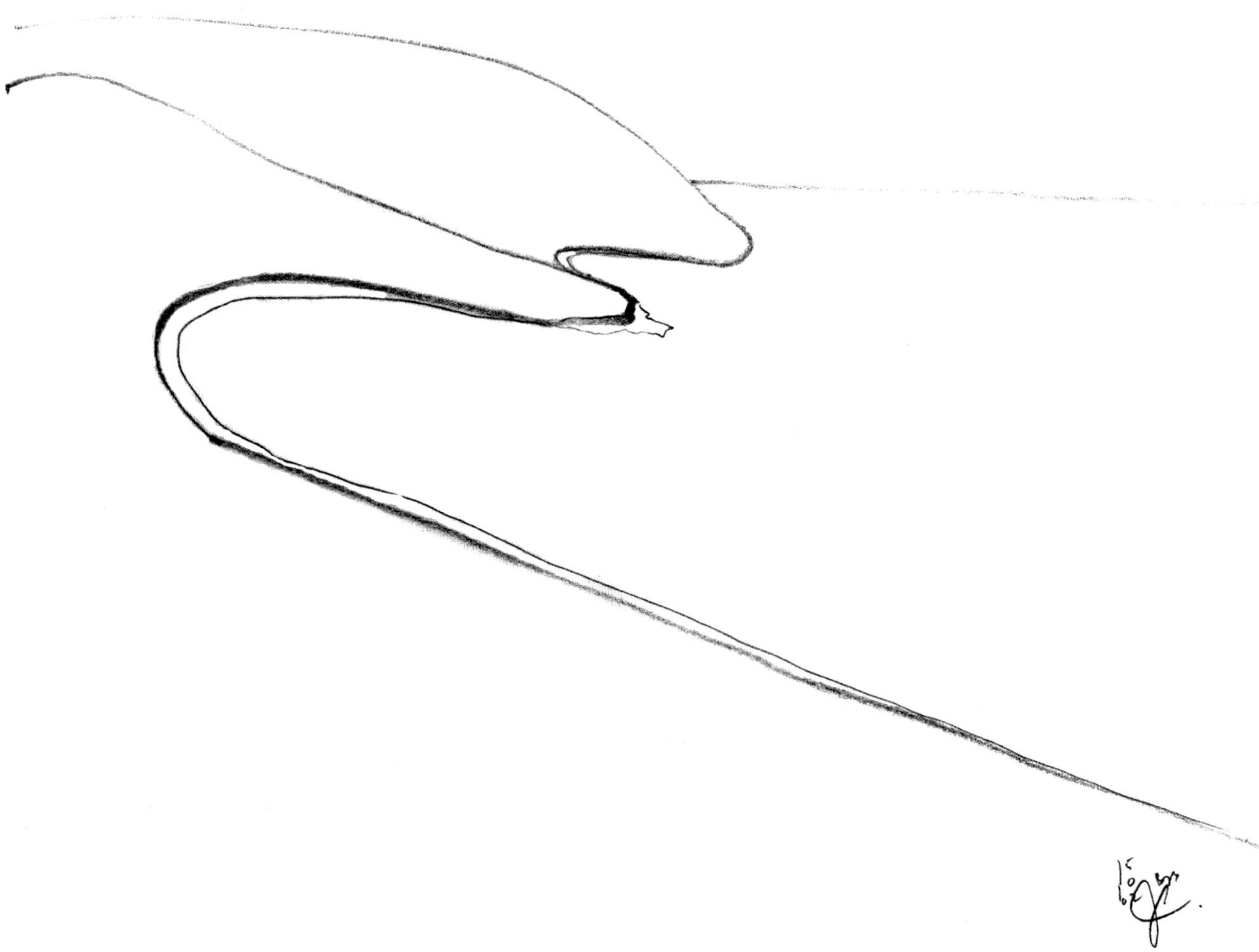

Bays beyond, the moving edge.

Ventilation and light.

Central stairway top to bottom – roofs define space. Thermal mass below.

Above:
Scale by roofs, view through, roofs light off roofs.

Next page:
View from street to bay beyond.

2002 — 2006
Newport, NSW, Australia

Beach House

The ground level of the Beach House integrates with the foredune of Newport Beach on Sydney's most northern peninsula. The proximity of the house to the sand and saltwater ensures that this is a place of both beauty and drama – a pavilion to shelter from the heat of coastal summers and a platform to survey the surf or passing seasonal squalls.

The mild climatic conditions of the area are translated through the architecture, to offer a dialogue on place and the interaction between occupant, landscape, architecture and climate. Space, closure and prospect define the rituals of the day, expressing the connection between the present and the past, the land and the platform.

Dune vegetation is robust and rigid – resisting erosion and relishing the salty breath of the ocean. Beach House is similarly robust. Tuning its environment for survival. Orientation responds to the prevailing winds, photovoltaic cells and an integrated floor heating system harness the sun. A misting pond cools space with captured rainwater. The house breathes and nurtures itself through it's own systems.

Early concepts for this building stipulated that occupants should be grounded 'within' the dune of shifting sands – to live on the ground, while sleeping in the sky. This grounding is achieved with a functional clear span area, with unusually high ceilings and a perimeter of operable walls. When the walls are peeled back fully, the only marker of the building edge is the transition from lightness to shade.

Above this level, a roof provides a canopy layer to protect a group of calm elevated rooms. With a wonderful elevated outlook to take advantage of the view, apertures from sleeping and washing spaces, reveal the garden and landscape beyond.

Each day this house resonates with the timelessness of the surrounding land and ocean, while referencing the traditional relationships between people, place and climate.

Location: Newport, Northern Beaches, NSW Elevation: 13m Prevailing winter wind: Southwest Prevailing summer wind: South, southeast, northeast Min temperature: +1°C Max temperature: +37°C Annual precipitation: 1219mm Design: 2002 – 2004 Construction: 2005 – 2006 Architects: Peter Stutchbury, Sacha Zehnder Engineers: Professor Max Irvine, Karl Mateiszika Landscape Architect: Ken Lamb, Phoebe Pape Builder: Bellevarde - John Fielding, Adam Howe

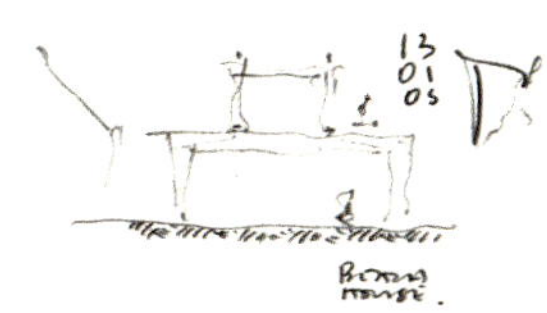

Early sketch illustrating the start of the house concept.

Left:
Existing Japanese garden preserved – entry stroll.

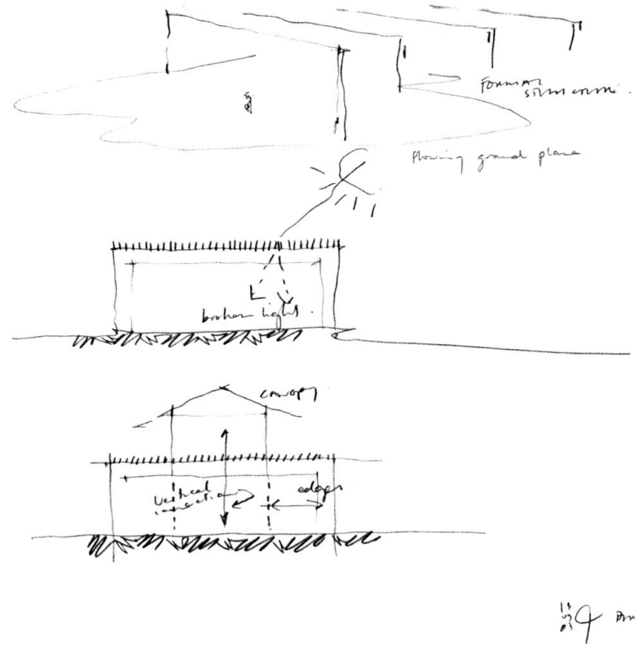

Making a place in the sand dune.

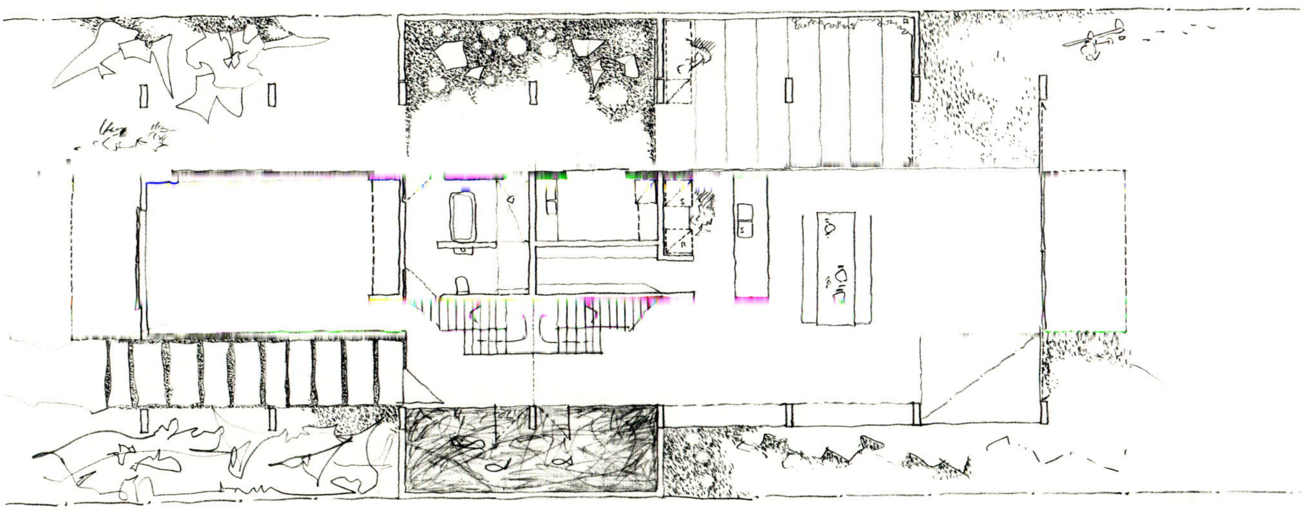

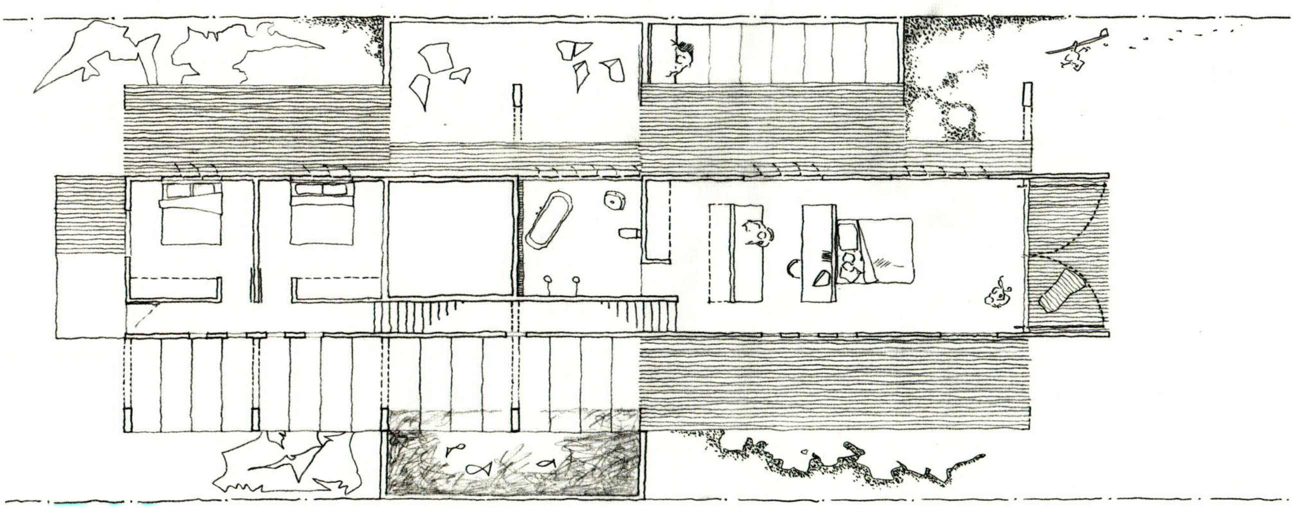

A Japanese client who encouraged clean lines and order.

Bedroom awakens to morning light.

Above:
Stair as free-standing sculpture in a masonry core.

Next page:
Building enclosure disappears.

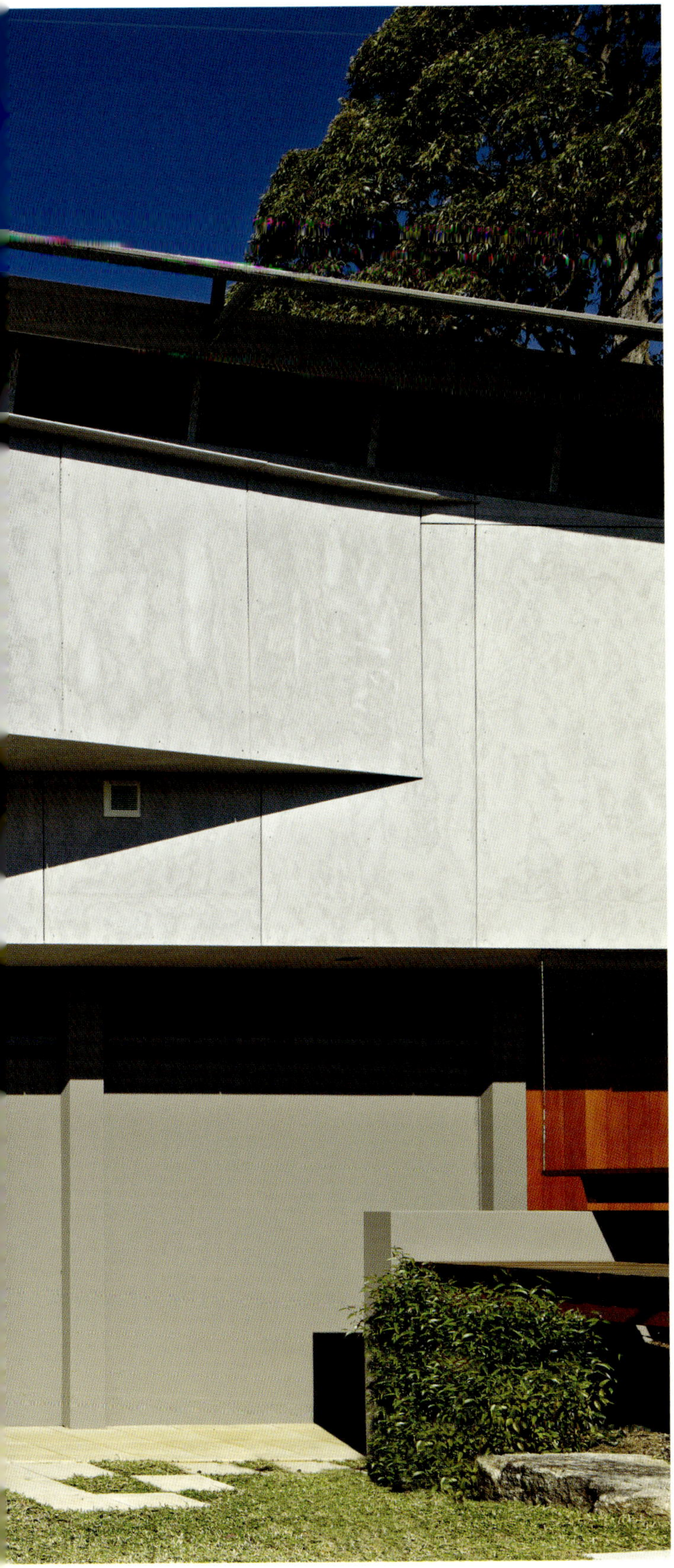

Previous page:
A careful facade and integrated garden links with the street.
Left:
A solid base with lightweight protected platform.

Original large opening bi-fold door and glimpse of coastline.

One single floating volume provides enough space for eating, resting, cooking and retreating from the sun.

This page:
Indoor / outdoor kitchen with a large retractable panel overhead.
Next page:
An indoor / outdoor 'wet' area is solid base for the platform.

2002 — 2007
Seaforth, NSW, Australia

Garden House

Garden House has emerged in two parts over 15 years. Initially the commission was for a studio located in the rear garden of a suburban 1970's home. This was the first deliberate effort on the part of the owners to prepare for the future disassembly of the main house. The studio still stands as a beautifully simple space – a testament to the timelessness of high quality precise timber construction.

In keeping with original intentions, the most recent layer to this project required a total remodelling of the existing 1970's house, as well as the design of a series of connecting elements between the two buildings and surrounding gardens.

Existing passage through and between the garden, studio and house was reinterpreted with a set of simple but functional pavilions, which blurred the formal and the informal, merging open garden, partial enclosure and enclosure in a layered, seamless living environment.

The new house lifts an eyelid to the north, allowing winter warmth to penetrate. Walls peel away to reveal gardens, and the gardens themselves become spaces for exterior living. A garden pavilion now houses formal dining, while a Frangipani courtyard becomes the wall between informal living and dining. The kitchen functions as a series of adjoining spaces, expanding the idea of 'room'.

Garden House is a legible step away from the concept of 'house' as we know it. It proposes that any suburban block of land can primarily be a landscape into which rooms are placed. When viewed as a whole, these make a place for dwelling. This project goes far beyond the proposition of glass or moveable walls as connection. It challenges historic references and searches for a more impermanent occupation of the land.

This house articulates the firmly held belief that homes should allow for liberty and flexibility between functions, and create an experience much like camping. Rooms should be spaces that remain connected to place and landscape, not limited by walls, but defined by roofs. These spaces can provide the needs for human habitation while leaving the spirit free to wander.

Location: Seaforth, Northern Beaches, NSW Elevation: 63m Prevailing winter wind: South, west Prevailing summer wind: South, south east, north east Min temperature: +3°C Max temperature: +39°C Annual precipitation: 1219mm Design: 2002 – 2003 Construction: 2006 – 2007 Architects: Peter Stutchbury, Rachel Hudson Engineer: Simon May and Associates Landscape Architect: Wendy Parker Builder: Builtform - Scott Hindmarsh

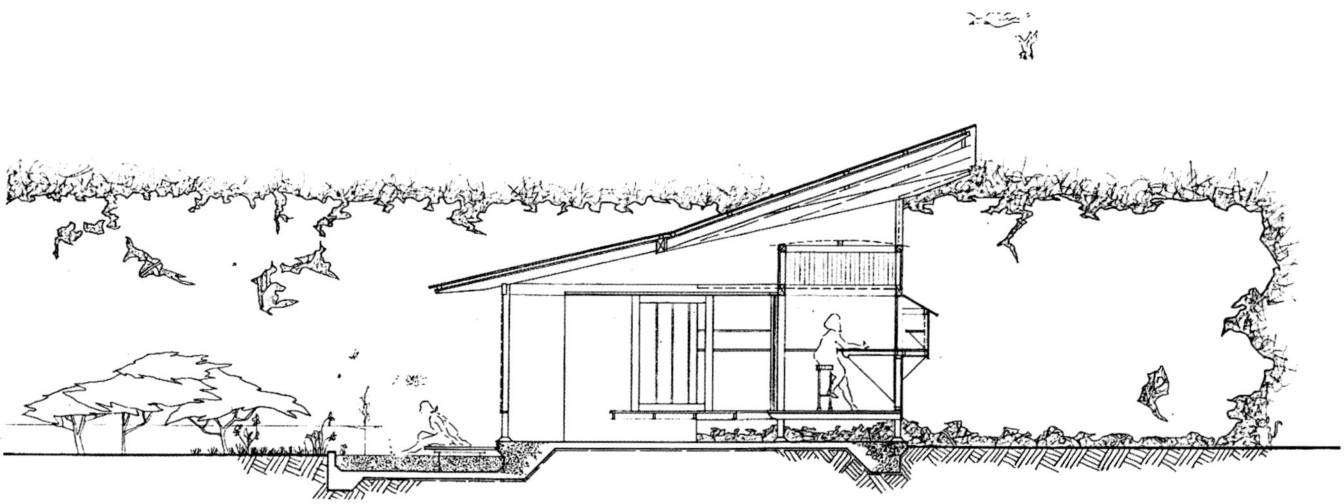

Original design studio.

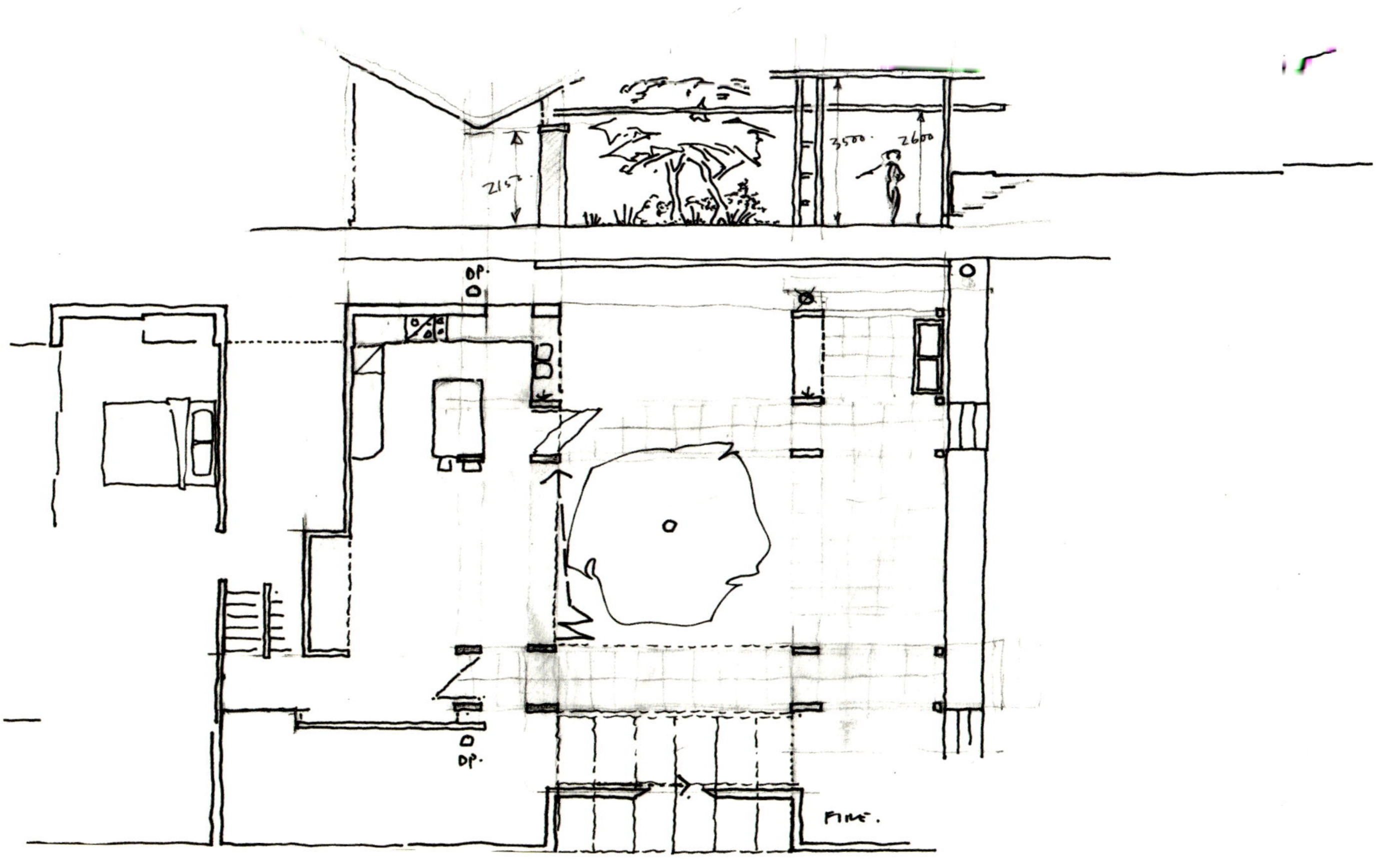

Above:
Garden connection.

Next page:
Terraces and a garden.

Stairway to studio, pond as wall.

2002 — 2004
Killcare Heights, NSW, Australia
Theatre House

Houses designed for Australia's coastline must inevitably respond to the harshness of the elements. Capturing the power of the landscape is however a more complex challenge. Amplifying the rawness of the heath and shoreline, sheltering from the heat and slanting light, capturing the dramatic scale of the ocean horizons.

This coastal house is located within an upmarket residential area at Killcare Beach on Sydney's Central Coast 90km north of the city. Internally it is a three-bedroom home designed for flexible living. Externally it seeks to find its own place within the heath.

A massive hardwood frame supports a simple over scaled canopy roof that provides necessary shelter. Blade walls beneath this canopy are punctured and cut to provide moments of privacy, shade, breeze and prospect. The eastern wall of the house is skewed to the view, to the north, full-height louvres that can open or close – blocking or emitting the sun allow for day to day flexibility.

The south wall, the direction of the harshest weather, has only one small opening to provide a morning view to the surf break. The glazed eastern facade frames the view, with large rising doors that open the interior to the landscape. Protected verandahs of varying sizes are placed along the edges of the building.

The theatricality of this house is as much defined by the setting as it is by the sculptural form of the building. Its large wall surfaces form an angular rhythm as they weave together to define the volume of the interior spaces. The house reinterprets the traditions of the coastal holiday house, while striving to maintain the essential rule that coastal living is about informality and space for the wandering mind.

Location: Killcare Heights, Central Coast, NSW Elevation: 90m Prevailing winter wind: Northwest Prevailing summer wind: Southeast Min temperature: +1°C Max temperature: +38°C Annual precipitation: 1315mm Design: 2002 Construction: 2003 – 2004 Architects: Peter Stutchbury, Richard Smith Engineers: Professor Max Irvine Builders: Glenn Cochran, Glen Boekeman

Previous page:
Structure against edge to landscape beyond.
Left:
The facade shifts to reveal and express the structure.

Operable louvres for winter sun and general light.

Above:
Large unencumbered opening to terrace and land.

Next page:
Subtle entry along timber colonnade.

2002 — 2004
Bayview, NSW, Australia

Verandah House

This house is situated on the south facing edge of a moist bushland valley north of Sydney. In winter the ground is damp and shaded, while in summer the place can be uncomfortably hot and dry with the only cool breeze high up in the trees. The land surrounding the house is shared by several families, as such any building needs to consider the privacy and outlook of neighbours.

In response to the primary concerns of coolness, heat and privacy, Verandah House is designed around a primary concrete platform that has been elevated towards the bush canopy. From this solid base the life of the house moves off both vertically and horizontally. The base also provides thermal mass for passive heating and cooling.

Controlled sunlight is drawn and reflected into the various interior spaces of the building between a long line of structural plywood fins that have been placed along a corridor wall. This corridor forms the emotional spine of the house, inviting light, colour and shadow in to play.

Lifting the building off the ground allows it to reach out to the breeze, to avoid dampness and to catch the winter sun, while also leaving the under-croft free as a shaded place for kids to play.

Verandah House experiments with the proposition that an open-walled, semi-exposed room, set under an extended canopy, is a more appropriate dwelling space for most Australian buildings than the traditional enclosed and mechanically cooled 'room' spaces that now predominate.

This warm and cool place, under the edge of the canopy, with access to cooking and washing facilities, is an idyllic, simple zone for living. It catches the sun and the breeze and welcomes the natural environment into the lives of the family who dwell here. Hovering amidst the tree canopy.

Location: Bayview, Northern Beaches, NSW Elevation: 33m Prevailing winter wind: South, west Prevailing summer wind: South, southeast, northeast Min temperature: +1°C Max temperature: +38°C Annual precipitation: 1219mm Design: 2002 – 2003 Construction: 2003 – 2004 Architects: Peter Stutchbury, Sacha Zehnder Engineers: Professor Max Irvine Builder: Pocklington Thornton

60

Covered room adjoining the cooking space.

Above:
Bounced light corridor serves the length of the house.

Next page:
The western facade of a verandah opens up to the forest.

2004 — 2007
Whale Beach, NSW, Australia

Outcrop House

Location: Whale Beach, Northern Beaches, NSW Elevation: 66m Prevailing winter wind: South, west Prevailing summer wind: South, southeast, northeast Min temperature: +1°C Max temperature: +37°C Annual precipitation: 1219mm Design: 2004 – 2005 Construction: 2005 – 2007 Architects: Peter Stutchbury, Richard Smith, Sacha Zehnder Engineers: Simon May and Associates Landscape Architect: Phoebe Pape Builder: Pocklington Thornton

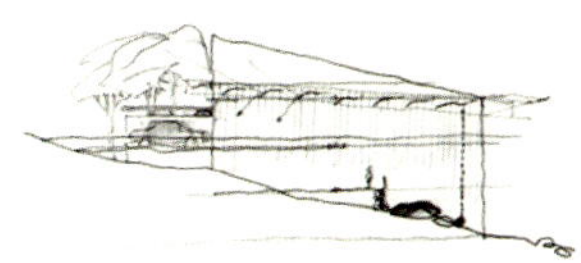

Sketch illustrating the means of filtering light through the roof to the interior.

The coastline of Sydney is typified by a landscape of stunning cliff-fringed beaches and rock platforms that rise dramatically from the surf to a high escarpment. The escarpment edge connects the saddles of bays with rocky headlands, forming a series of natural amphitheatres that vault along the coastline.

This sandstone escarpment edge, exposed to the salt and wind was once the traditional walking edge for Indigenous people; providing both prospect and a structure for navigating the landscape.

Outcrop House is sited in such a place, a sandstone escarpment edge facing due south over bush, beach and ocean. An ephemeral rivulet connects the site both physically and emotionally to the beach below. Prevailing winds from the south accelerate across the beach, searing up over the escarpment edge, giving this place a rugged quality. A primary challenge was to resolve the southern aspect with access to northern winter sun.

As with many of Sydney's populated ocean edges this place is a point along the final line between suburbia and wilderness, irreversibly connected between urbanity and landscape.

Capturing this rawness, a single large-scale aperture opens from the house over Whale Beach to the south. The opening, and hence the prospect of the site, is theatrically staged through a series of frames, accessed from the platforms and volumes of the house.

The roof canopy and exterior wall structures form one primary room into which secondary interior elements have been placed. The roof slopes up to the north allowing solar access in winter and consists of a layering of curved timber elements below a triple skin polycarbonate skin, which allows light to filter and refract into the interior, filling the house with a magical shifting light.

Responding to its south-facing aspect, a winter courtyard defines the northern perimeter of the house. For additional thermal control, the house has been recessed into the escarpment, locking it into the land amongst this soft sedimentary geology.

In keeping with the simplicity of the place – heath, rock, sand and wind – the building is restrained and subtle, an enclave that offers comfort and a constant sense of placement.

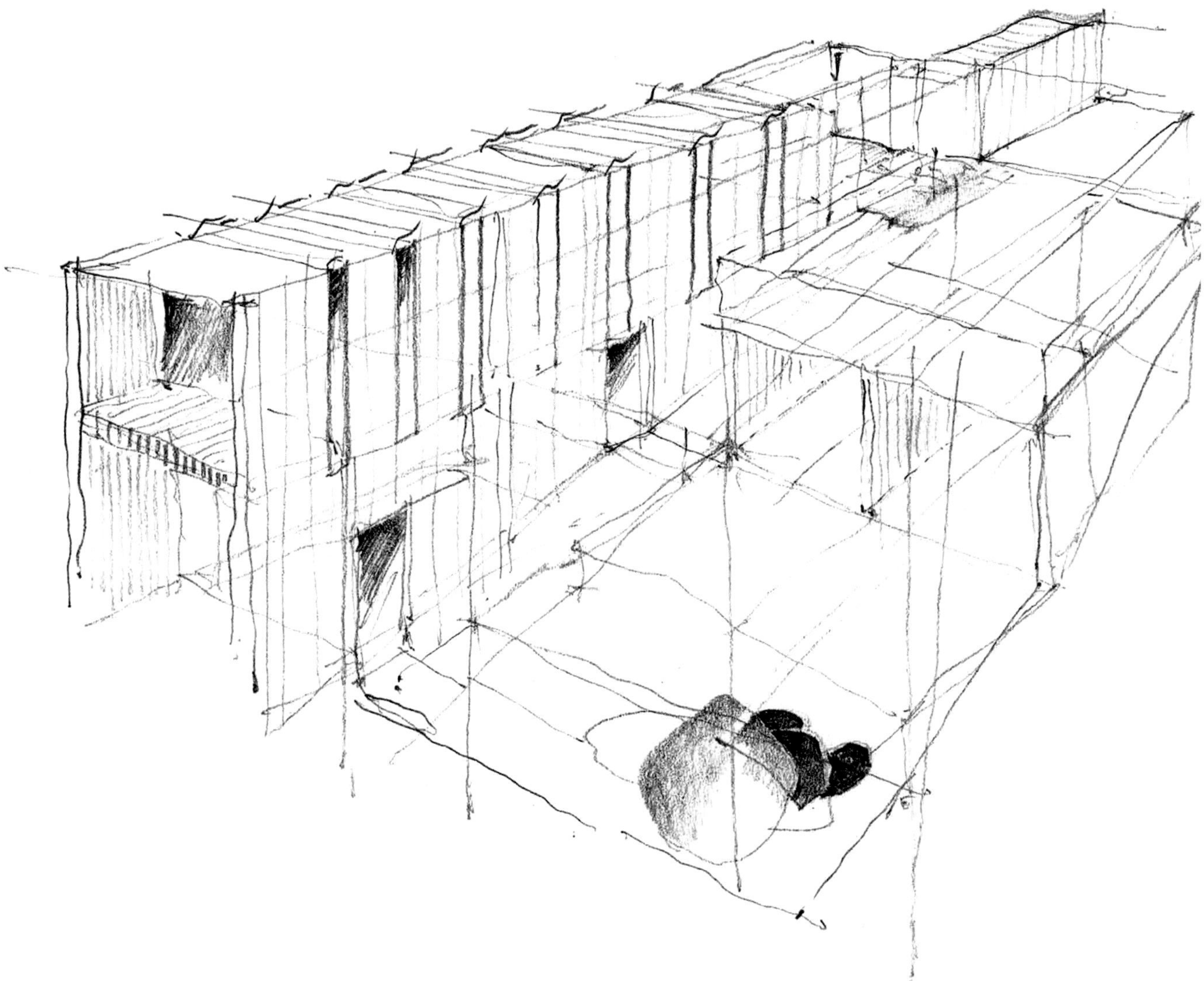

Sketch illustrating preliminary thoughts
that were refined to the final concept.

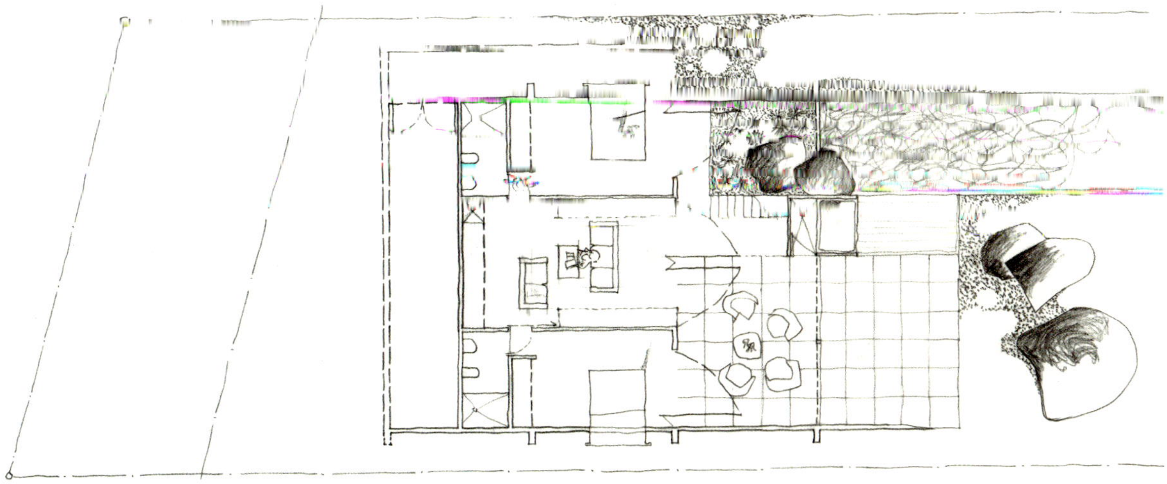

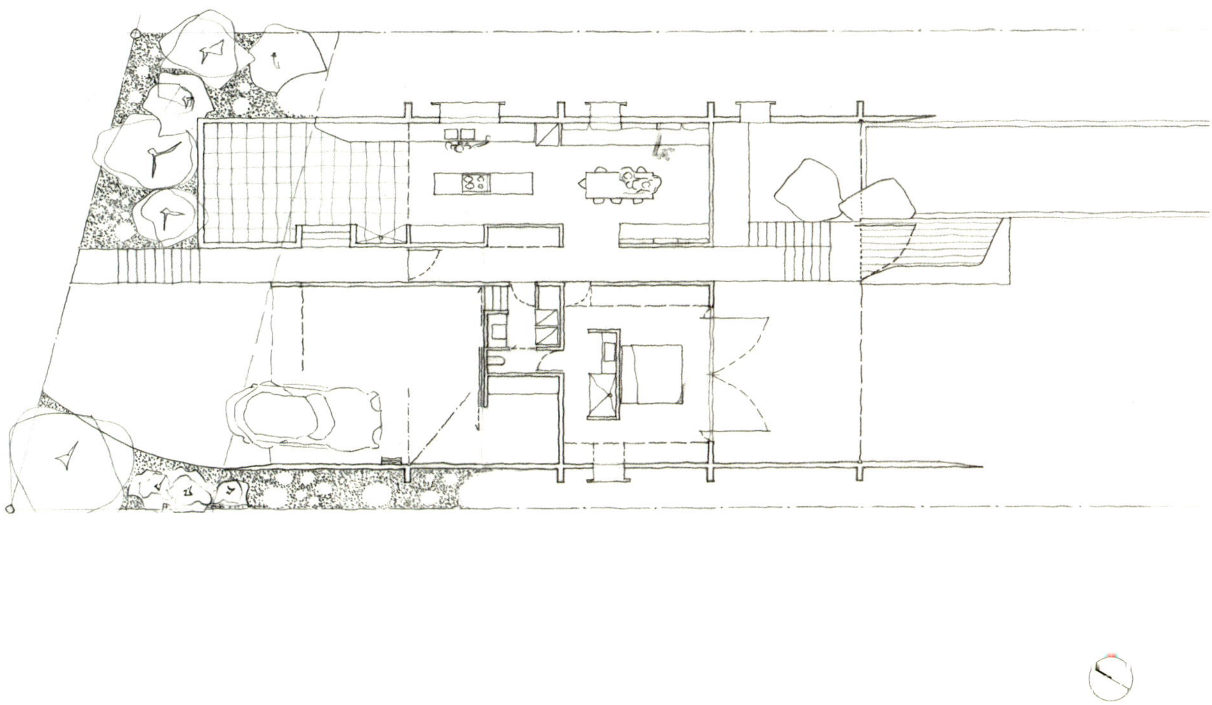

Next page:
Rooms without boundaries integrate interior and exterior experiences.

Light flows from apertures in the ceiling, modulated by plywood panels. A 'window' serves as a display space.

An open vertical space connects the house with the beachscape beyond. Walls are adjustable for privacy or to access the view.

A long functional kitchen connects to the outside via an opening, linking to the view beyond.

Intermediate space stretches to the headland. An external bed is provided.

Above:
Thermal mass and cave like sleeping rooms.

Next page:
Pool connects to the ocean and provides cooling for the house.

2005 — 2009
Cessnock Aerodrome, Hunter Valley, NSW, Australia

Hangar Flying Museum

Hangar is a gallery, museum and operational facility for a collection of historic aircraft. The building performs both as a tourist attraction and functional hangar.

Responding to the theatrical presence and scale of the aircraft, the building is designed as a technically sophisticated yet romantic enclosure with sufficient volume to provide for the movement of aircraft. Hangar is essentially utilitarian, yet offers visitors a memorable 'aeronautical' experience.

Much of the drama within the design derives from the powerful arc of its cantilevered wall and roof, casting the building forwards to float across the runway. The curved southern facade invokes the form of World War Two 'blister' hangars – vaulted structures designed to be invisible from the air.

Reminiscent of a wing profile, which gains maximum strength from minimal material, the form of the building is a highly efficient single skinned structure. The integrity of the structure is maintained through the use of 15m spans of Aramax roof sheeting locking the building together between the four main trusses of the primary structure. The curved vault truss is engineered to 'spring' support the 12-meter cantilever awning. This extends beyond a clear span 30m-door, providing unobstructed access and weather protection between the working interior and the taxiway. This structural system initiative has produced a net steel tonnage reduction of 30%.

Administration 'pods' are affixed on the east and west facades of the building: east for entry, west for outlook. These points are connected via a 45m suspended walkway, which acts as a central east-west axis and viewing platform for the building.

The hangar is a well-planned and serviced volume, which is economical and environmentally responsible, while creating a theatrical public window into aviation history.

Location: Cessnock Aerodrome, Hunter Valley, NSW Elevation: 64m Prevailing winter wind: Northwest Prevailing summer wind: South, southeast
Min temperature: -1°C Max temperature: +40°C Annual precipitation: 700mm
Design: 2005 - 2007 Construction: 2007 - 2009 Architects: Peter Stutchbury, Matt Markham-Lee Engineers: Simon May Associates Landscape Architect: Phoebe Pape Builder: Babic Construction – Tony Babic

A sculptural landscape.

Late afternoon light.

Above:
Generous column-free space.

Next page:
Building and plane together.

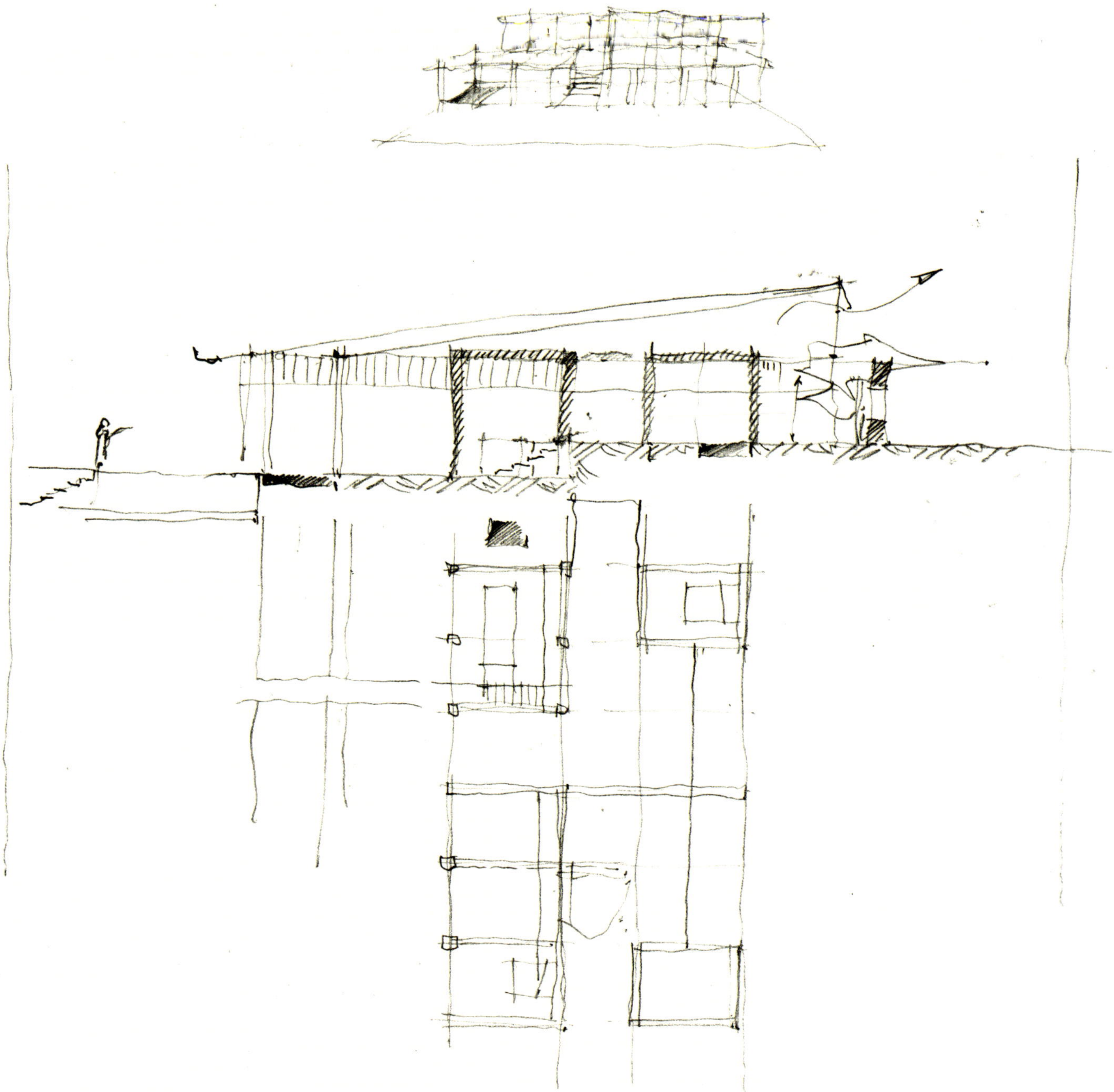

Sketch illustrating air flow from ocean.

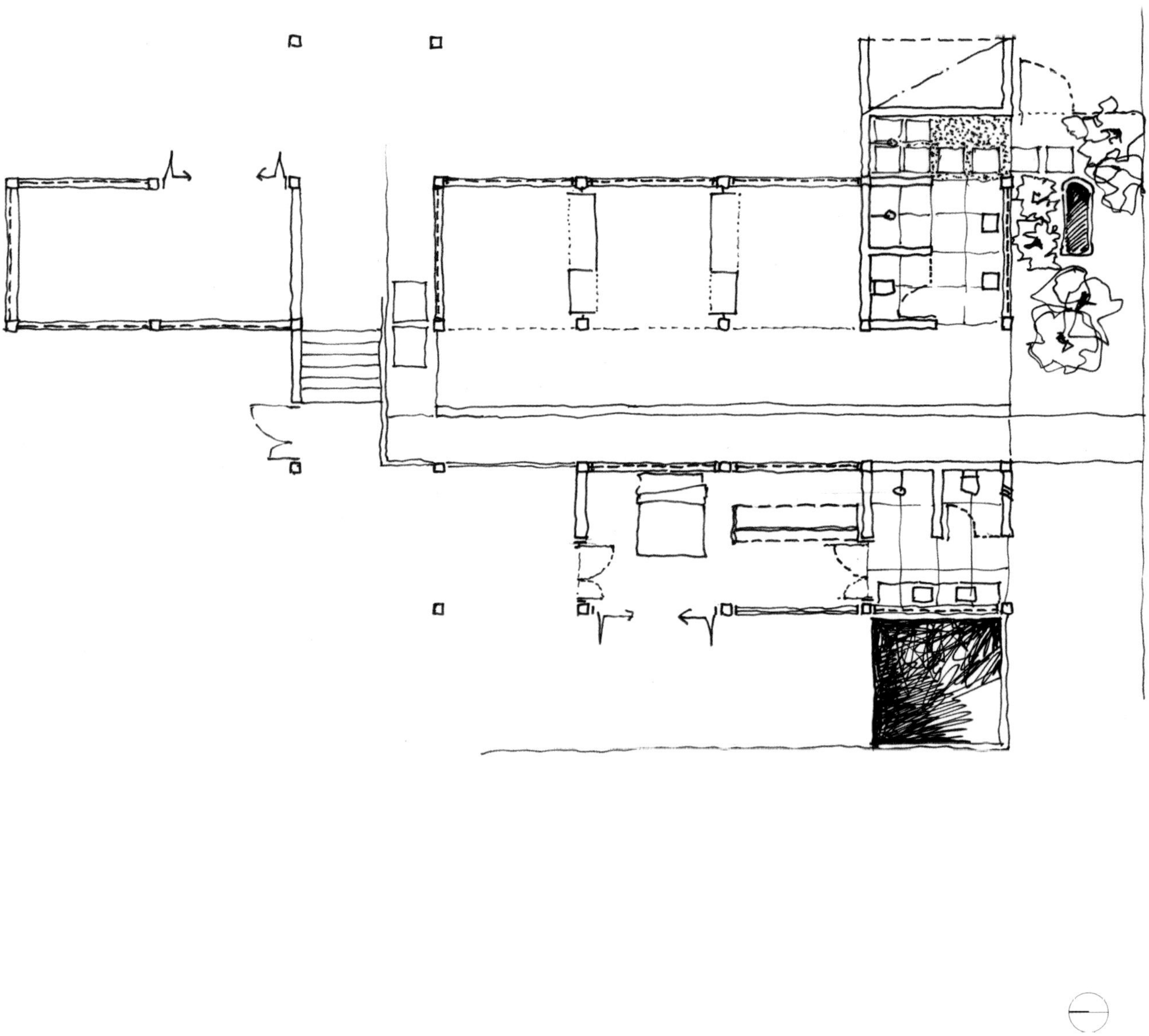

The strength of a regular grid.

Cyclone frames in the landscape.

Next page:
The simple expression of overhang for protection, frame for strength, infill for purpose.

A channel brings the sound of water inside the house and provides additional cooling.

A house tuned to a tropical lifestyle.

Left:
Sleeping rooms integrate with the gardens.
Next page:
Utilitarian bathrooms.

2006 — 2011
Berry Mountain, NSW, Australia

Contour House

Contour House provides a living environment set somewhere between the formality of home and the informality of camping.

Located 30km from the New South Wales coast; just below the lip of a long spur of land that connects the coastal hinterland of Berry with the rim of the stunning escarpment fringed Kangaroo Valley. The site is cold in winter and hot in summer, with hot dry winds and potential bushfires from the west.

The house is in many ways a barometer of the local climate, designed to be open to the elements in fine weather or sealed down at extreme times of the year – in the depth of winter and height of summer.

Set against the contours of the land the house hugs the slope; a heavy masonry wall forms a perimeter to guard against fire and hot wind from the west whilst also protecting a series of cool southern courtyards for use in summer.

Lifting out of the slope, the house facilitates varying levels of connection back to the land. Interior spaces frame the view from different perspectives, establishing a sense of location and placement in the landscape. Where the house joins the ground a variety of physical touch-points allow seamless movement between interior and garden. A series of semi-enclosed in-between spaces provide connection to the elements, use of each space depends on the time of day, the ambient temperature and prevailing wind.

Contour House heats and cools itself through a variety of passive means, with thermal mass, cross ventilation, geothermal air, evacuated tube and solar penetration maintaining a comfortable internal environment all year round.

With a total internal area of 232sqm this small building provides a range of independent spaces for three families who share. A central living zone provides communal space, while independent bathrooms and sleeping spaces connected by a tube structure provide separation, the tube provides an extension to other interior spaces.

Location: Berry Mountain, Southern Highlands, NSW Elevation: 292m Prevailing winter wind: West, northwest Prevailing summer wind: South Min temperature: 0°C Max temperature: +36°C Annual precipitation: 1860mm Design: 2006 Construction: 2009 – 2011 Architects: Peter Stutchbury, Nichole Darke, Pietro Chiefa Engineers: Professor Max Irvine Landscape Architect: Phoebe Pape Builder: Wilcon Building - Gavin Williams

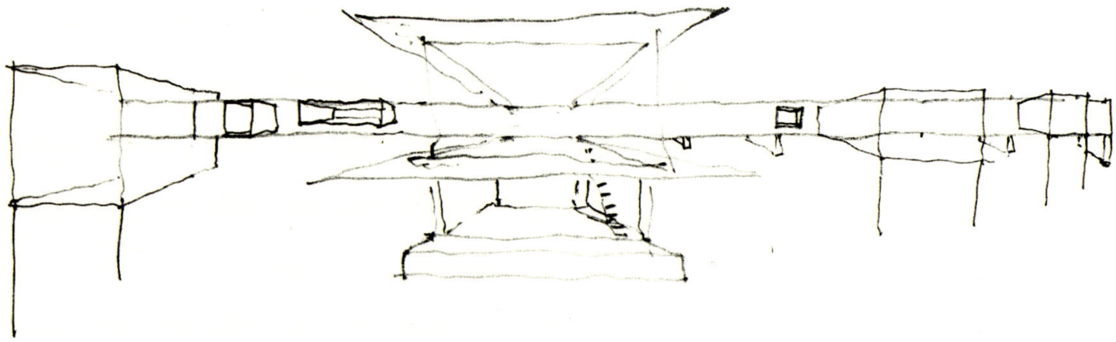

Early sketch describing the house as courtyards,
and demonstrating the flow of space.

Next page:
The Contour House stretches toward the eastern horizon.

This page
Living room amongst the trees.

Next page:
The thermal gallery serves the eastern rooms over the valley floor.

2007 — 2011
Palm Beach, NSW, Australia
with Fergus Scott Architects

Cliff Face House

Pittwater is a large saltwater estuary north of Sydney that opens dramatically onto the mouth of the Hawkesbury River at Broken Bay. The area is a haven for sailing, fishing and boating, and as such the land surrounding the bay is coveted for its proximity to the water and the city.

Located on the eastern edge of Pittwater, this house makes the most of a potentially complicated site that drops steeply more than 10m from the main road to the shoreline below. Despite the challenges, this small parcel of land, neatly tucked into the elbow of a shimmering bay, offers a wonderful place to live just across the water from a National Park.

Traditionally the residences in this area have been placed on a narrow flat area of land adjacent to the road, sitting above a small cliff face. This placement ignores the drama of the location, perching houses away from the water with their backs against a road.

Breaking with convention, this house embraces the challenge of the site as a creative opportunity. Harnessing the beautiful terrain and texture of the cliff, a series of layered planes, built against the exposed sandstone cliff wall; drop the house away from the road. An upper level entrance courtyard is connected to the shore via a central staircase that runs through the house.

This house is designed as a place of ease, where a retired couple can live on a self contained upper level. Lower levels provide direct access to the waterfront and serve to accommodate visiting family and friends.

Construction is robust and economical, based upon a series of elegant scaffold platforms anchored into the cliff. Primary elements are repeated to enable efficiency, including steel walkways and operable facade panels.

On the lower two levels, the cliff face threads through the interior along a circulation spine, merging hand hewn stone with manufactured glass, concrete and steel.

Providing passive climate control, a double, or 'fly', roof acts as a shading canopy over a curved opaque polycarbonate sub-roof and upper walls. Operable perforated panels slide together to shroud the facade from the hot western afternoon sun. The glass clad central staircase doubles as an operable thermal chimney – retaining heat in winter and releasing it in summer. Similarly the cliff is harnessed as a source of passive summer coolness, with floor apertures drawing air across the cool stone into the house.

Location: Palm Beach, Northern Beaches, NSW Elevation: 33m Prevailing winter wind: South, west Prevailing summer wind: South, southeast, northeast Min temperature: +1°C Max temperature: +37°C Annual precipitation: 1219mm Design: 2007 – 2008 Construction: 2009 – 2011 Architects: Peter Stutchbury, Fergus Scott, Caryn McCarthy, Linda Markham-Lee, Nichole Darke, Rachel Hudson Engineers: Professor Max Irivine Landscape Architect: Phoebe Pape Builder: State Construction Group - Sam Deriu

Protected eastern courtyard looking onto
'fly-roof' structure.

Protected eastern courtyard with covered
outdoor dining area and lap-pool

Cliff face bathroom.

Operable facade panels running the full length of the western façade retract and adjust to control privacy and shading.

2005 — 2011

Blue Mountains, NSW, Australia

Invisible House

Invisible House is a simple sculptural form that strives to be in harmony with its surroundings – to disappear. Construction materials are sympathetic with the area. The water-covered roof reflects the ever-changing sky.

The house is located on the western edge of the Blue Mountains, part of Australia's Great Dividing Range. The house faces east, out over expansive mountains and bush.

Exposure to the elements is a defining characteristic of this location, with weather ranging from constant summer sun and scorching westerly winds, to petrifying cold winter winds from the valley and ranges.

The design team used a three-day camp to test possible locations for a house, moving slowly around the site to consider the impact of this exposure on a dwelling.

From four potential locations, the final choice of site was reinforced through evidence of earlier use as a grazier's shelter. These observations then informed the design of a house which positively embraces the harsh elements.

Tucked below the brow of a hill and dug into the contours of the site the house anchors itself within the flow of the ridge, reducing height and exposure, while also minimising aesthetic impact in the landscape.

The plan emphasises the placement of the house in the landscape, optimises the dramatic horizon to the east and filters direct light reaching the interior.

This design is the outcome of a methodical examination of the local and distant landscape and climatic conditions, drawing together narratives about location, weather, and landscape to offer a story of belonging.

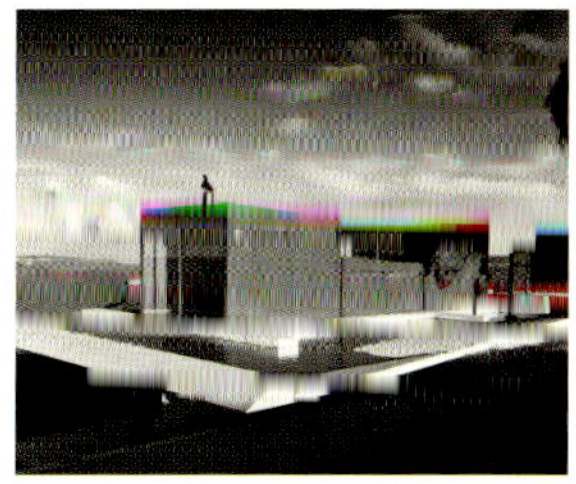

-- Location: Blue Mountains, NSW Elevation: 1170m Prevailing winter wind: Westerly Prevailing summer wind: South Westerly Min temperature: -8.2°C Max temperature: +36.6°C Annual precipitation: 762mm Design: 2008 – 2009 Construction: 2009 – 2010 Architects: John Bohane, Emma Neville, Richard Smith, Sacha Zehnder Engineers: Max Irvine Builder: Dimark Construction

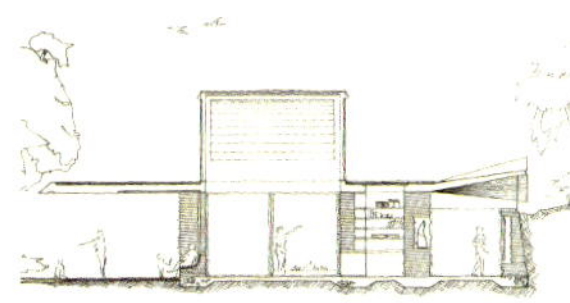

-- East-west section looking south with glazed box on the roof for daylight.

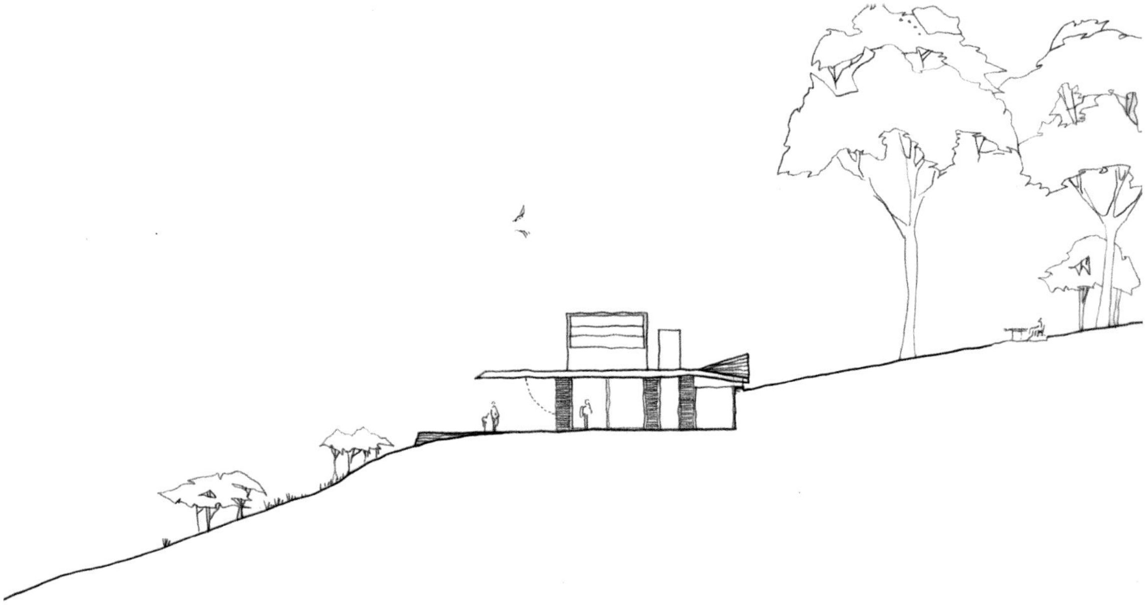

Sketches showing the placement of the house recessed into the hillside.

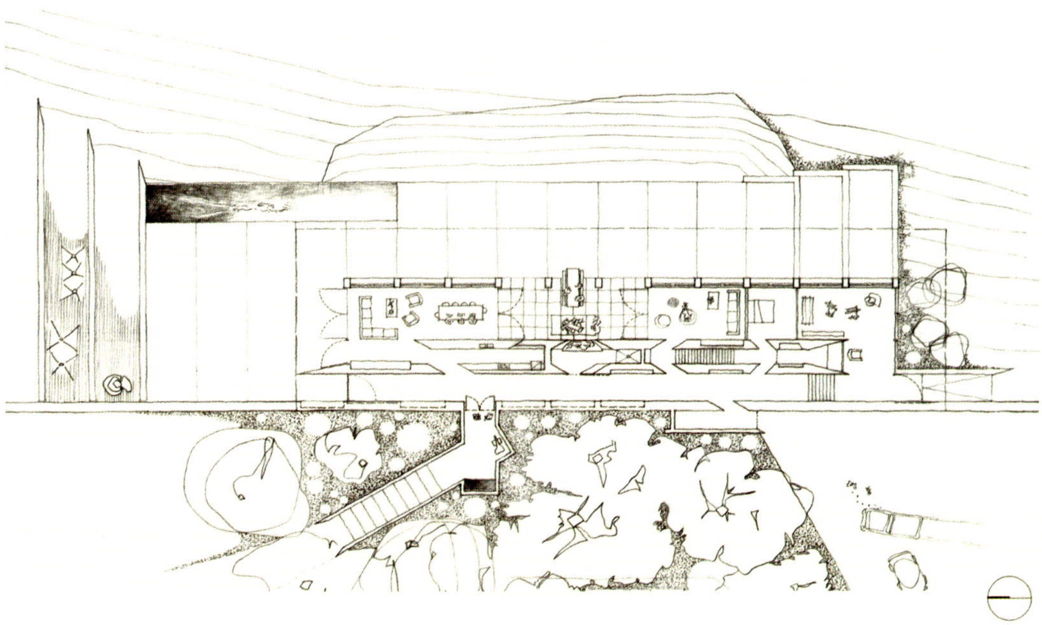

Sketched floor plans with contours. Upper level with master bedroom, water covered roof and skylights. Lower level with entrance tunnel, covered courtyard and northerly terrace.

Previous page:
Looking east the house slots into the hillside, reducing exposure to the prevailing winds.

This page:
View from the north into main living area with elevated glazed box to catch the sunlight.

Curvilinear timber ceiling providing
access to northern light.

11th model.

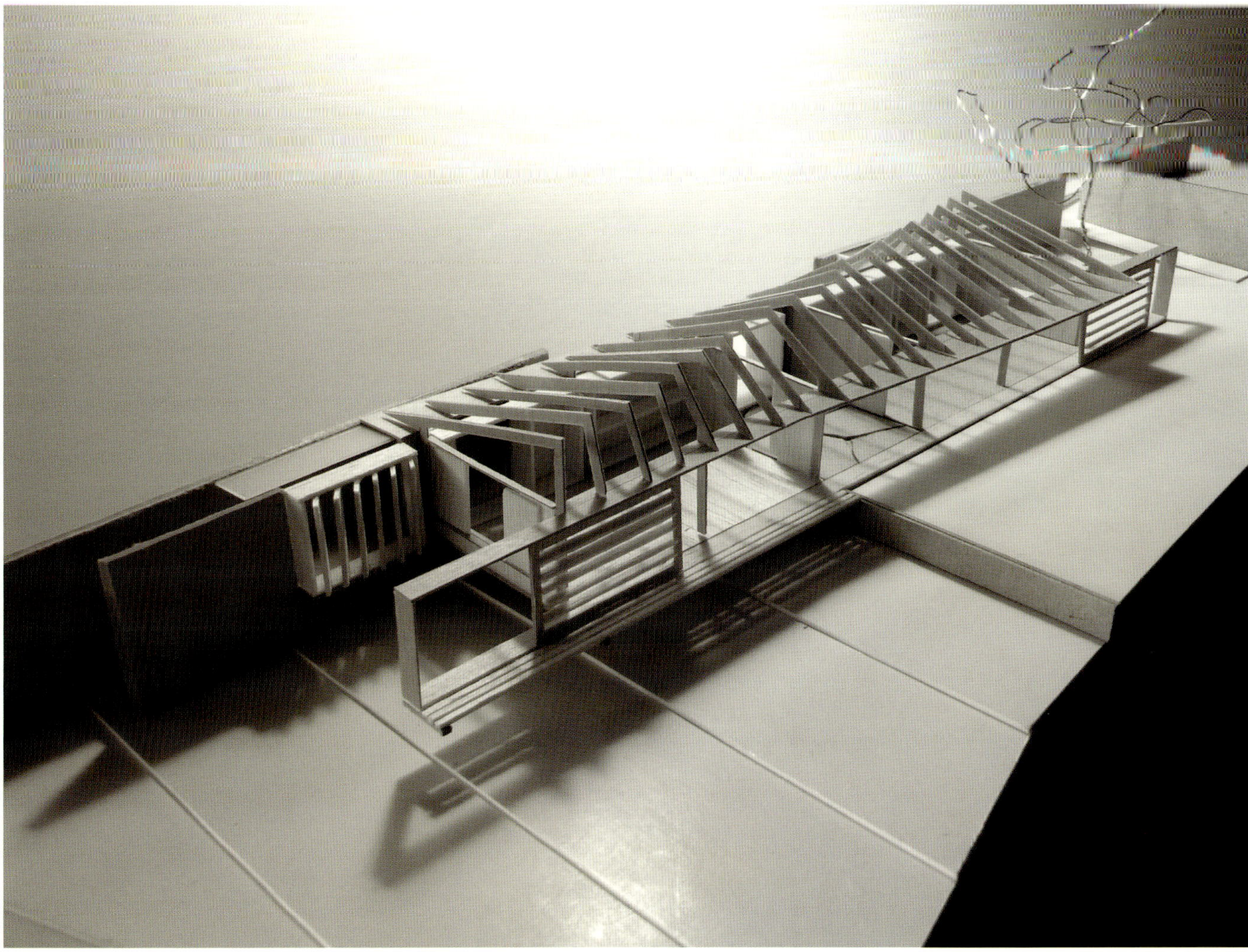

Reviewing the twisted roof through model making.

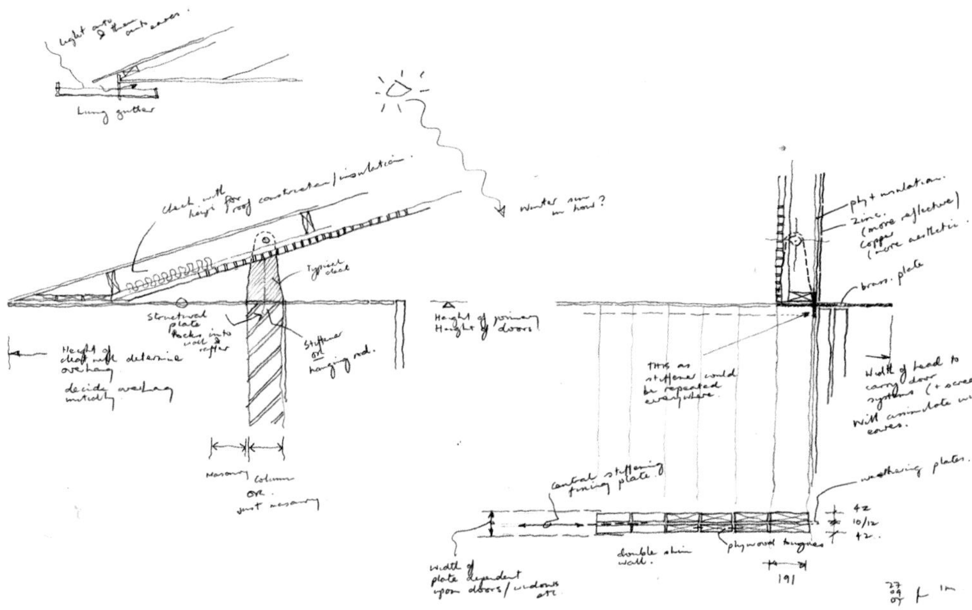
living gutter
winter sun on hood?
ply + insulation
zinc (more reflective)
copper (more aesthetic)
brass plate
Structural plate
Height of primary
Height of doors
This as stiffener could be repeated everywhere
central stiffening fixing plate
weathering plates
42
10/12
42
double skin wall
plywood tongues
191
Width of plate dependent upon doors/windows etc

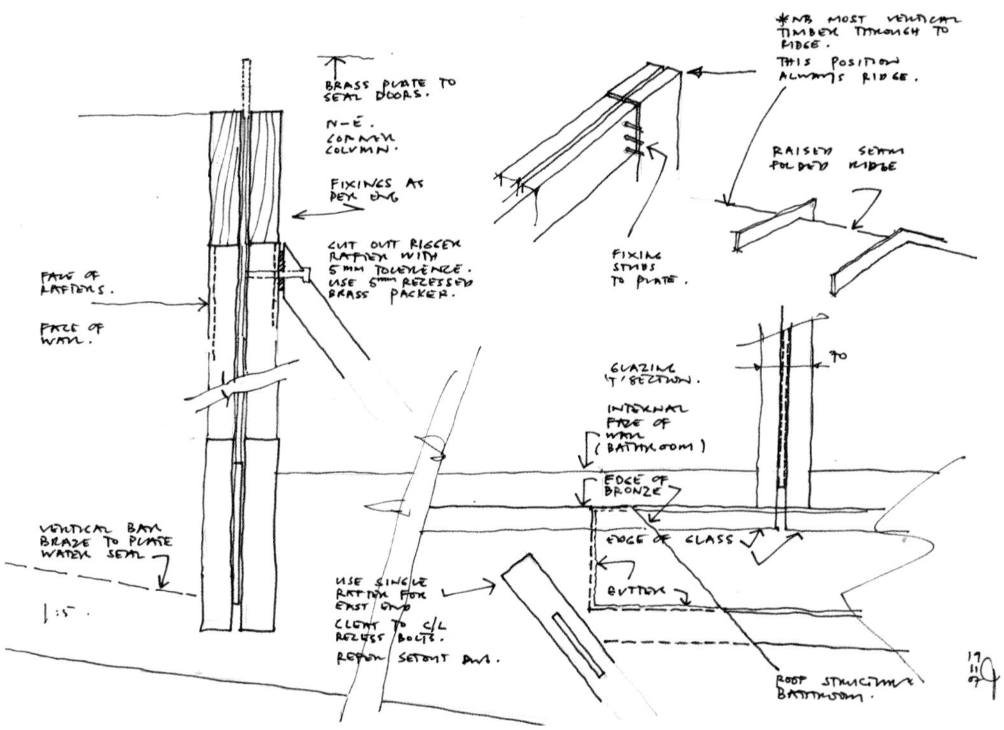
*NB MOST VERTICAL TIMBER THROUGH TO RIDGE.
THIS POSITION ALWAYS RIDGE.
BRASS PLATE TO SEAL DOORS.
N-E. CORNER COLUMN.
FIXINGS AS PER DWG
CUT OUT BIGGER RAFTER WITH 5 MM TOLERENCE. USE 5mm RECESSED BRASS PACKER.
FACE OF RAFTERS.
FACE OF WALL.
RAISED SEAM FOLDED RIDGE
FIXING STUBS TO PLATE.
GLAZING 'T' SECTION.
INTERNAL FACE OF WALL (BATHROOM)
EDGE OF BRONZE
EDGE OF GLASS
VERTICAL BAR BRAZE TO PLATE WATER SEAL
1:5
USE SINGLE RAFTER FOR EAST END
CLEAT TO C/L RECESS BOLTS.
REFER SETOUT DWG.
ROOF STRUCTURE BATHROOM.

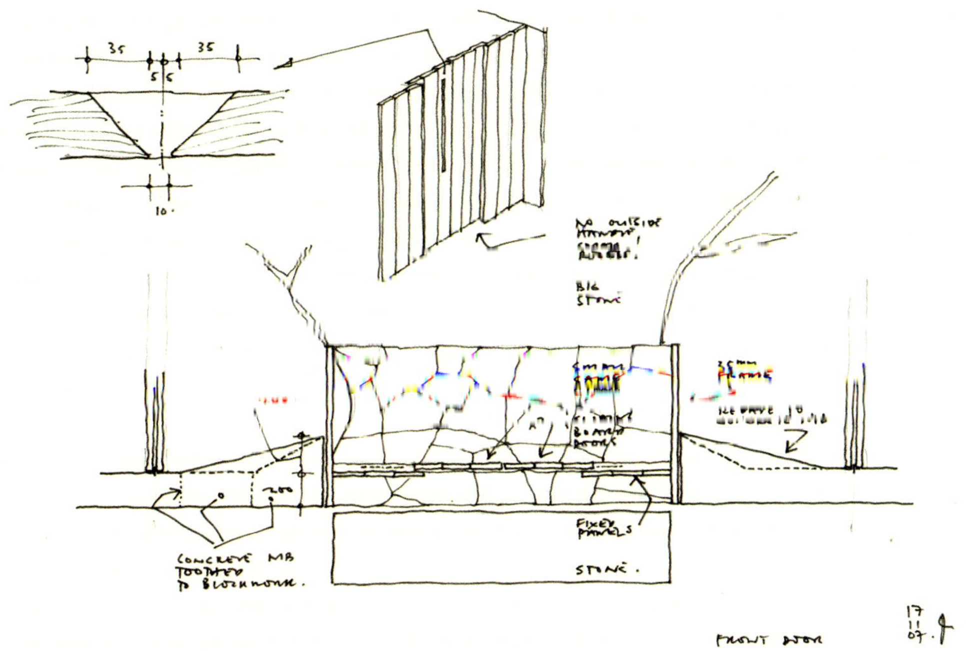

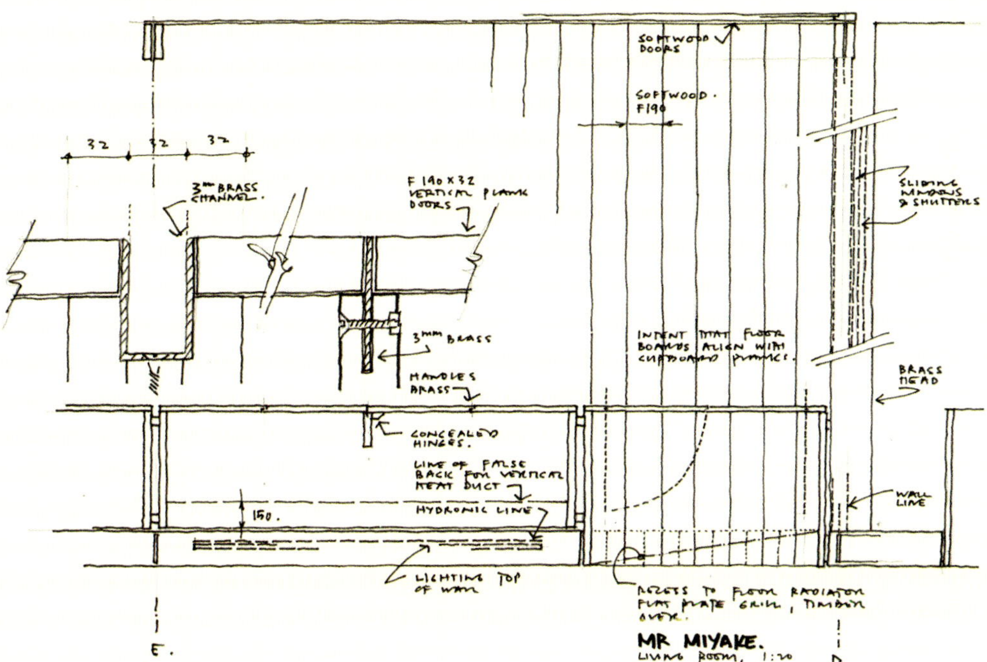

Left & Above:
House details.

Next page:
Site meeting, client, architect, friends.

Previous page and this page:
Rear view of the house showing the wall
to the street and entry ramp.

Entry area with vegetated screening to the street and sliding entry panels.

The main living zone of the house opens to garden and connects to the adjacent traditional house.

A covered room with an integrated element of water reflects the sky into the interior, connecting house, garden and sky.

A secure service corridor runs through the house below the diagonal ridge of the roof.

Diagonal connections from the house to the site with the roof floating above.

Room for rest.

A study looks onto a cherry tree and a small contemplation garden.

Above:
The roof follows the flow of the land.

Next page:
The house leans toward ocean, inviting morning light into the bathhouse.

Bathhouse.

A singular wall of retractable screens in the closed position.

House and garden combine, ocean and house connected

1978 — Peter Stutchbury Architecture **Project Index**

Stunted Spotted Gum, 2011

Aboriginal Housing, 1978
University of Newcastle, NSW, Australia
—
Peter Stutchbury

Pergola, 1979
Five Dock, NSW, Australia
—
Peter Stutchbury

Bunk house & shearer's quarters, 1979
Cobar, NSW, Australia
—
Peter Stutchbury

Castlecrag Addition, 1980
Castlecrag, NSW, Australia
—
Peter Stutchbury, Shelley Indyk

Church, 1982
Port Moresby, Papua New Guinea
—
Peter Stutchbury

Home Addition, 1982
Avalon, NSW, Australia
—
Stutchbury's

Nick & Carol Gilbert House, 1983
Moorland, NSW, Australia
—
Peter Stutchbury

Primmer Residence, 1983
Bermagui, NSW, Australia
—
Peter Stutchbury

Van Pelt Residence, 1983
Gosford, NSW, Australia
—
Peter Stutchbury

Mary Gilbert Residence, 1984
Burrell Creek, NSW, Australia
—
Peter Stutchbury

West Head House, 1985 – 1991
Clareville Beach, NSW, Australia
—
Peter Stutchbury, Phoebe Pape

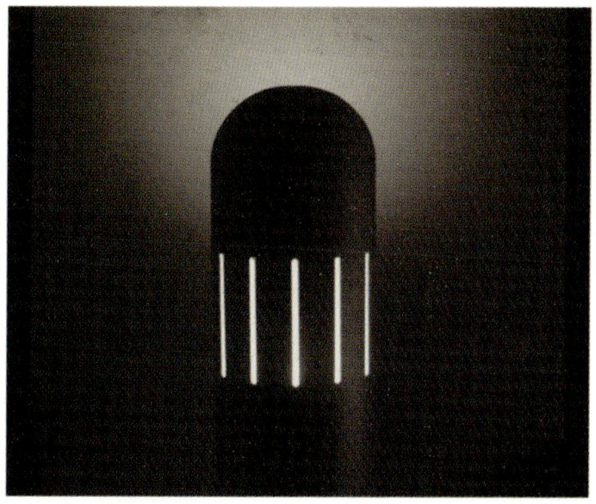

Lamp, 1986
—
Peter Stutchbury

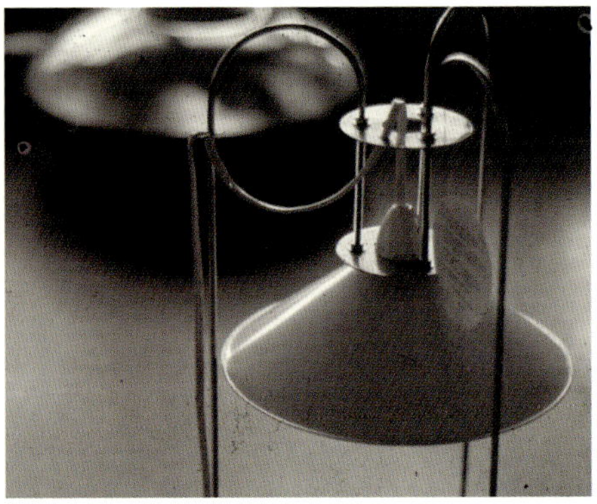

Lamp, 1986
—
Peter Stutchbury

Israel House, 1986 – 1992
Paradise Beach, NSW, Australia
—
Peter Stutchbury
—
Timber Design Award: Commendation - RAIA NSW (1993);
Merit Award: Residential - RAIA NSW (1995);
Commendation Robin Boyd Award - RAIA National (1995)

Mark/Greville Residence, 1986
Bawley Point, NSW, Australia
—
Peter Stutchbury

Brown Residence, 1987 – 1992
Bilgola Beach, NSW, Australia
—
Peter Stutchbury, Anne Commeaux
—
Timber Design Award: Commendation - RAIA NSW (1994)

Hudson Pavilion, 1988
Avalon, NSW, Australia
—
Peter Stutchbury, Anne Commeaux

Montessori Kindergarten, 1988
Avalon, NSW, Australia
—
Peter Stutchbury

Campbell Addition, 1988
Bungendore, NSW, Australia
—
Peter Stutchbury

Treetop House, 1991
Clareville, NSW, Australia
—
Peter Stutchbury

Bethungra Park Stables, 1991
Wagga, NSW, Australia
—
Peter Stutchbury

Pape Residence, 1991
Crows Nest, NSW, Australia
—
Peter Stutchbury

Selby/Booth Addition, 1991
Woollahra, NSW, Australia
—
Peter Stutchbury, Fergus Scott

Martin Addition, 1991
Lindfield, NSW, Australia
—
Peter Stutchbury

Bay House, 1996 – 2000
Watson's Bay, NSW, Australia
—
Peter Stutchbury, James Stockwell
—
Residential Architecture Award - RAIA NSW (2003);
Robin Boyd Award - RAIA National (2003)

Jane Prior Addition, 1996
Avalon, NSW, Australia
—
Peter Stutchbury, Sue Harper

SMS Visitor's Centre Project, 1996
Snowy Mountains, NSW, Australia
—
Peter Stutchbury, Fergus Scott

Kangaroo Valley Pavilion, 1996 – 1998
Kangaroo Valley, NSW, Australia
—
Peter Stutchbury, Sacha Zehnder
—
Timber Award - RAIA NSW - Country Division (1999);
Domain People's Choice Award - RAIA NSW (2000);
Australian Timber Design Awards - Overall Winner (2000)

Sydney International Archery Park, 1996 – 1999
Homebush Bay, NSW, Australia
—
Peter Stutchbury, Katrina Julienne, Fergus Scott
—
Public Buildings Award - RAIA NSW (1999);
BHP Colorbond Award - RAIA National (1999);
Award of Excellence - National Metal Industries (1999)

Cliff House, 1997 – 2001
Newport Headland, NSW, Australia
—
Peter Stutchbury, Marika Jarv

Birabahn - with Richard Leplastrier & Sue Harper, 1996 – 2002, University of Newcastle, NSW, Australia

—

Peter Stutchbury, Richard Leplastrier, Sue Harper, Shane Blue, Richard Smith

—

Blacket Award - RAIA NSW (2003); Public Building Architecture Award - RAIA NSW (2003); Sir Zelman Cowen Award - RAIA National (2003); Prime Minister's Banksia Environmental Award (Newcastle University) (2004)

Reeves House - with Sue Harper, 1997 – 1999
Clareville Beach, NSW, Australia

—

Peter Stutchbury, Sue Harper

—

Residential Architecture Award - RAIA NSW (2000); Domain People's Choice Award - RAIA NSW (2000); Commendation Robin Boyd Award - RAIA National (2000)

Life Sciences Link Building - with Suters, 1997 – 2001
University of Newcastle, NSW, Australia

—

Peter Stutchbury, Dino DiPaolo, Matt Markham-Lee, Fergus Scott, Brian Suters, James Fraser

—

Prime Minister's Banksia Environmental Award (Newcastle University) (2001); Sir John Sulman Award - RAIA NSW (2001)

Hendry/Taylor House, 1998 – 2003
Canberra, ACT, Australia

—

Peter Stutchbury, Judith Phillips

—

Architecture Award - RAIA ACT (2004)

Springwater, 1998 – 2005
Seaforth, NSW, Australia

—

Peter Stutchbury, James Stockwell

—

Award for Architecture: Single Housing - RAIA NSW (2005); Robin Boyd Award – RAIA National (2005)

Wedge House, 1999 – 2001
Whale Beach, NSW, Australia

—

Peter Stutchbury, Marika Jarv

Glade House, 1999 – 2002
McMasters Beach, NSW, Australia
—
Peter Stutchbury, Richard Smith, Fergus Scott

Harbour House, 1999 – 2003
Newcastle, NSW, Australia
—
Peter Stutchbury, Shane Blue
—
Architecture Award - RAIA NSW (2004)

Bangalay, 2000 – 2005
Upper Kangaroo Valley, NSW, Australia
—
Peter Stutchbury, Marika Jarv
—
Award for Architecture: Single Housing - RAIA NSW (2006); Blacket Award - RAIA NSW (2006); Commendation Robin Boyd Award - RAIA National (2006)

Depot Beach House, 2000 – 2007
Depot Beach, NSW, Australia
—
Peter Stutchbury, Richard Smith

Furniture, 2000
Depot Beach, NSW, Australia
—
Peter Stutchbury, Richard Smith

Paddock House, 2000 – 2007
Tarago, NSW, Australia
—
Peter Stutchbury, Sacha Zehnder

Deepwater Woolshed, 2000 – 2005
Wagga Wagga, NSW, Australia
—
Peter Stutchbury, Sacha Zehnder
—
Blacket Award - RAIA NSW (2005); Award for Architecture: Commercial Buildings - RAIA NSW (2005); Award for Architecture: ESD - RAIA NSW (2005); Colorbond Award - RAIA NSW (2005); Commercial Award for Architecture - RAIA National (2005); Colorbond Award - RAIA National (2005)

Hill House, 2001
Central Tilba, NSW, Australia
—
Peter Stutchbury

Cole Addition, 2001
Roseville, NSW, Australia
—
Peter Stutchbury, Rachel Hudson

Between 2 Valleys, 2001 – 2004
Kangaroo Valley, NSW, Australia
—
Peter Stutchbury, Marika Jarv

The Vision, 2001
Bungan Beach, NSW, Australia
—
Peter Stutchbury, Grant Mears

Verandah House, 2002 – 2004
Bayview, NSW, Australia
—
Peter Stutchbury, Sacha Zehnder

Beach House, 2002 – 2006
Newport Beach, NSW, Australia
—
Peter Stutchbury, Sacha Zehnder

Theatre House, 2002 – 2006
Killcare, NSW, Australia
—
Peter Stutchbury, Richard Smith

Garden House, 2002 – 2007
Seaforth, NSW, Australia
—
Peter Stutchbury, Rachel Hudson
—
Architecture Award – AIA NSW (2008)

Avalon House, 2002 – 2007
Avalon, NSW, Australia
—
Peter Stutchbury, Marika Jarv, Rachel Hudson
—
Architecture Award – AIA NSW (2008)

Bay Beyond, 2003 – 2006
Killcare, NSW, Australia
—
Peter Stutchbury, Richard Smith

Nader Addition, 2003
Tuross, NSW, Australia
—
Peter Stutchbury, Rachel Hudson

Paradise View, 2003 – 2006
Avalon, NSW, Australia
—
Peter Stutchbury, Marika Jarv

Outcrop House, 2004 – 2007
Whale Beach, NSW, Australia
—
Peter Stutchbury, Richard Smith, Sacha Zehnder
—
Australian Timber Design Award – Overall Winner (2008); Architecture Award – AIA NSW (2009)

Cardboard House, 2004
Opera House Forecourt, NSW, Australia
—
Peter Stutchbury, Richard Smith, Matt Markham-Lee, Col James, with Ian Buchan Fellowship
—
Special Jury Award - RAIA NSW (2005)

Coogee Addition, 2004 – 2006
Coogee, NSW, Australia
—
Peter Stutchbury, Matt Markham-Lee

The Hangar, 2005 – 2009
Cessnock, NSW, Australia
—
Peter Stutchbury, Matt Markham-Lee

Invisible House, 2005 –
Hampton, NSW, Australia
—
Peter Stutchbury, Sacha Zehnder, Richard Smith, Emma Neville, John Bohane

Peter Stutchbury Architecture
Studio

Ameé Allsop

—

Studio

—

Belinda Koopman

—

Barbecue

—

Eleri Smith

—

PSA team in 1999

—

Helen Mackay

—

Studio

—

John Bohane

—

Picnic
—

Nielsen Warren
—

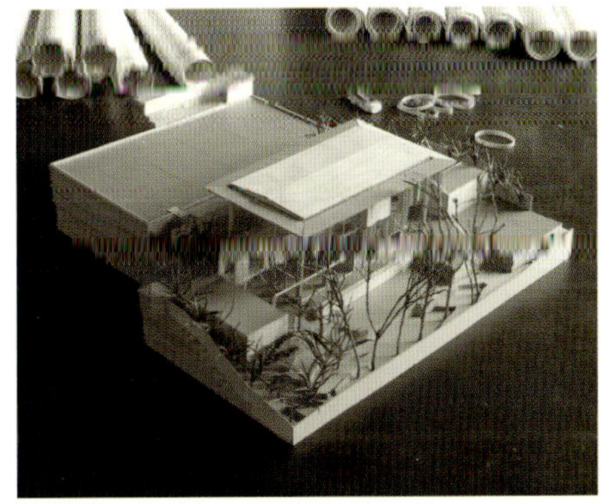

Model
—

Bronte Stutchbury
—

Studio
—

Studio verandah
—

Rachel Hudson
—

Studio
—

Peter Stutchbury
—

International competition design session

—

Friday lunch

Jennifer McMaster
—

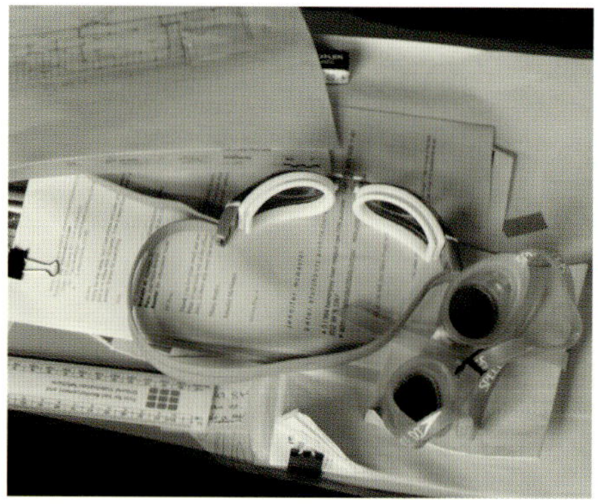

Studio
—

Matt Markham-Lee
—

Studio
—

Professor Max Irvine
—

Studio
—

Nic Moore
—

Studio
—

Nichole Darke
—

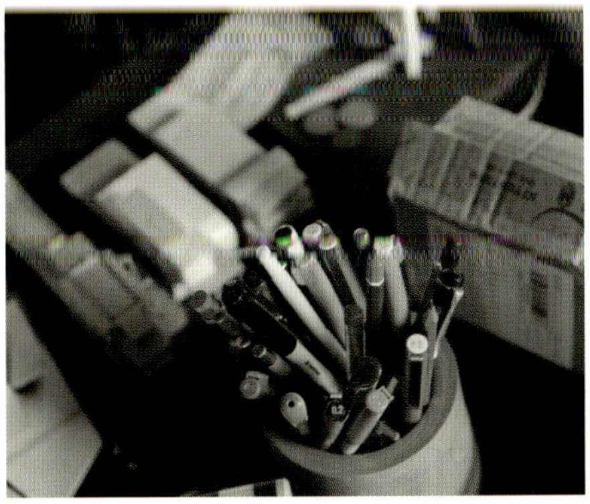

Studio
—

Site visit
—

Richard Smith
—

Studio verandah
—

Ulrika Saar
—

Studio
—

Julie Fraenkel
—

Studio
—

Yuki Kajigaya
—

The Architecture Foundation Australia would like to acknowledge:

Peter Stutchbury and his staff for their wonderful architecture and the effort they put in to make material available for this book.

Photographer:
Michael Nicholson for his commitment to accurately capturing and representing the many buildings featured in this publication.

Editor:
Ewan McEoin at Studio Propeller

Graphic designers:
Michaela Webb and Mike Giesser at Studio Round.

Contributors:
Brit Andresen, Ingerid Helsing Almaas, Richard Leplastrier, Peter Stutchbury

The many staff who have worked alongside Peter through the years:
Ameé Allsop, Kota Arai, Maria Aragao, Ann Bassett, John Bohane, Leni Borg, Casey Bryant, Vanessa Carnevale, Genni Castelli, Jocelyn Cheu, Pietro Chiefa, Anne Commeaux, Sam Crawford, Nichole Darke, Federica De Vito, Julie Fraenkel, Rachel Hudson, Sue Harper, Marika Jarv, Paul Johnson, Kira Jovanovsky, Katrina Julienne, Yuki Kajigaya, Shiku Kamugi, Belinda Koopman, Helen Mackay, Matt Markham-Lee, Laura Dewe Mathews, Caryn McCarthy, Jennifer McMaster, Grant Mears, Franziska Militz, Nic Moore, Charlotte Nelms, Emma Neville, Phoebe Pape, Chris Patterson, Claudia Pickering, Karina Piper, Adriano Pupilli, Ulrika Saar, Fergus Scott, Martina Shelley, Eleri Smith, Richard Smith, James Stockwell, Bronte Stutchbury, Jonathan Temple, Nielsen Warren, Sacha Zehnder, Josh Zuenert

In association:
Keiji Ashizawa Design, Bourne & Blue, EJE, Ray Fitzgibbon, Col James & The Ian Buchan Fell Housing Research Unit, Sue Harper, Professor Max Irvine, Richard Leplastrier, Judith Phillips Architects, Fergus Scott, Suters Architects

Note from Peter Stutchbury:

We are fortunate to work alongside highly creative and talented people. Sincere thanks to Lindsay Johnston for producing this book. With respect we recognise Phoebe Pape for her wonderful contribution and Professor Max Irvine for his integrated and inventive advice. I acknowledge the work of all persons noted within project details, the builders and their teams who make ideas come to life – consultants Jim Olive and Craig Burton who work intimately with our team to improve results and those architects who have by their involvement made the Projects in Detail thoroughly better works of architecture. In particular I thank Richard Smith. Ingerid Almaas for her written vision and Richard Leplastrier for time shared. Michael Nicholson for his remarkable skills. Our clients are our heroes – they take journeys that beforehand were foreign by nature. They occupy buildings with understanding and they put trust in our ability to create. It is in fact equally their work.

ARCHITECTUREFOUNDATIONAUSTRALIA